Some Dogs Are Angels

Typeset, printed, and bound in Canada.

Dedications

This book is dedicated to Murray, Colleen and Wanda:

Murray whose unquestioning and unfailing generosity ensures that our dogs never go hungry. We struggle to find the words to express our gratitude.

Colleen and Wanda, without whose generous and selfless intervention, it would have been another two years before this book came to print.

To Victoria, Jasmine and Michelle: Thank you so much for keeping our pack fit and healthy. Your never ending kindness and tolerance of our impecunious state is humbling. We could not wish for our beloved animals to be looked after by a more caring and giving veterinary team, or a more supportive and gentle a group of people.

We would also like to offer our grateful thanks to those others who have provided invaluable support and assistance along this journey: our best-in-the-world neighbours, Scott and Shannon; our good friend and counsellor, Jane; our spiritual fellow travellers Angie, Diego and Wayne whose company it is such as joy to be in; my ever loving parents who accept everything we do and everything we are and are always there for us. Thank you all.

Finally, to Susan, Karen, Rhaean, Joanne, Katy and all those many others out there who we have never come across in the world of dog rescue: You are truly wonderful, kind and good people. We are in awe of your work and hope that someday we may be of as much service as you.

This is a book about dogs.

It's also a book about a voyage of spiritual discovery.

On one level it is the story of how a family comes to find themselves sharing their house and their lives with nineteen dogs (so far).

It's also about how they come to discover that twelve of those dogs are avatars, the earthly embodiment of angelic beings.

And one is something else quite different.

Preface

Most people who meet me conclude that I am a very 'down-to-earth' person. Some would use the term 'grounded'. Others may even use less kind terms. But in essence they would agree that I am a practical, level-headed, realist. I'm very forthright, even blunt at times. If you're trying to persuade me of anything, you'd better have your ducks all in a row because I can be a tough audience to convince.

I'm neither prone to flights of fancy nor daydreaming.

I'm quite bright. I did a law degree, studied hard to get a Masters later in life and I have a Mensa measured IQ of 166.

Career wise I have spent the last twenty five years as both employee and employer in the field of human resource development.

I'm something of an expert on the subject of 'real' leadership and my book on the subject was the number two business bestseller in the UK some years ago.

I set up and ran an international people development business and created a series of software products that sold for an outrageous sum of money.

These are my credentials for being considered normal.

I'd also like to tell you that I'm an honest person. I treat others with respect and expect to be treated that way in return. I consider myself to be a man of honour and my word is my bond.

Everything that I am about to tell you is true.

Much of it will strike you as strange, possibly very strange. But it's all true.

People hear things when they're meant to hear them. They are drawn to information because it has meaning for them in that moment and for their future lives.

If you're reading this now, there is a very good chance that this is just such a moment for you.

There is a greater purpose in reading this book than the dog story you might have thought it was.

If you're not ready for it, simply go through the book without reading the text that is contained in the boxes that are dotted throughout the story.

But when you are ready, read it all. You're meant to.

I know this because I've been told it's true and I believe the person who told me.

He's an Archangel.

In the beginning...

In 1997 I had no knowledge of what an avatar was or even that such things existed, so how could I possibly have known that I had willingly invited one into my house? If I had known at the time all that would transpire as a result of this seemingly chance event, or been aware of the unfathomable implications that were being brought into play, I may have paused to reflect on the wisdom of allowing it all to begin. More likely, I would simply not have believed that such things were possible. And even if I had given it a moments credibility I would probably have gone into denial that they could affect me and my family. Nevertheless, come the avatar did, inexorably changing our lives forever. But I'm getting ahead of myself...

The story should really begin somewhere in my childhood since I had grown up in a home where a cat ruled. That is to say, our only pet was a Siamese cat, who although delightful and enchanting was no angel. I would not say that dogs were actively disliked, but my mother greatly favoured felines to the exclusion of all other creatures, and we didn't really know that many people with dogs.

The only 'significant' owner amongst these was my paternal grandmother who owned a very sweet and devoted miniature Poodle called Peri (pronounced pee-er-ree). On the rare occasions that we went to visit, we always received the most rapturous welcome from this little bundle of love. As a young boy I would always want to take Peri for a walk and she was a willing companion; until she realised that Gran wasn't coming too. Then she would try to pull me home, whining until I dragged her so far away from home that she realised there was no hope but to go on. On being reunited with her mistress she was overjoyed, even if we had only been away for a few minutes. She slept at the foot of Gran's bed and accompanied her everywhere. It was a picture to see Gran sitting in an armchair with the dog at her feet, just staring up at her adoringly. Her eyes never left her beloved owner's face.

When Gran made her bi-annual trips to South Africa to visit with her daughter, Peri couldn't go. In hindsight I am sure that a great deal of the pleasure of her trip must have been marred by her grief at having to leave the dog behind. The trips, often by boat, took months at which time Peri stayed with a friend. I don't think Gran would ever have left her with us, partly because she wouldn't have wanted to impose on the cat dominated household and partly because she knew that we would not have cherished her. Although Peri was a moderate distraction, for the most part we were indifferent to her.

I look back in shame now when I remember hearing that Peri was dead. Gran had shared her life with her for 15 years and knowing how much they adored one another, I now see that she must have been heartbroken when Peri died. Back then, as an unintentionally callous teenager, I greeted the news without concern, assuming that she could 'just get another dog'. But Gran would never share her life with another animal. She lived for 20 years after Peri's death and would most definitely have valued the companionship; yet she refused to replace her, saying that she was afraid that she would outlive the animal and that she couldn't bear the thought of a pet becoming homeless. She didn't really factor in her own needs, and the love and camaraderie that she shared with the little Poodle were never to be repeated. I guess on the larger scale of things it's only a very minor and very personal tragedy; nevertheless, in the maturity of adulthood I came to regret how blasé I had been about her loss. It would take the passing of two and a half decades, long after they had both passed away, before I would have the opportunity to make amends. But more about this later.

The childhood experiences of my wife Sharon were wholly different from mine. She loved dogs but had grown up in a house where pets were simply not welcome. Her maternal grandmother had dogs that she preferred to humans and Sharon has memories of her sitting on her porch, surrounded by her loyal companions. To the day she died she revered them and valued their company above all others. By contrast, Sharon's mother was fairly neutral with regard to animals. Her indifference most likely stemmed from owning a spaniel as a young girl that she adored. The animal died in awful circumstances and from that day onward, she seemed to seek to inure herself from the pain of the loss by rejecting animals as dirty and too much work.

The attitudes of the parents seldom seem to stop a child from craving animal company and Sharon was no exception. Almost by way of consolation, she had once been allowed to own a budgerigar called Trixie who was apparently enchanting. The bird was no less richly rewarding for in relationship terms than the spaniel had been for her mother. Although it is now over thirty years ago, Sharon still mourns the loss of Trixie and will recall her passing with grief that is as fresh and painful today as it was then.

However, her parent's final word on the subject of pets was "When you have your own house you can have as many animals as you like". How prophetic.

Having grown up in a house dominated by cat love and having a wife who would welcome any animal, it seemed perfectly natural to me that when Sharon and I decided to get a pet shortly after we married, we chose to get a Siamese cat. Actually, we came back with two, the last two of the litter. We couldn't really afford them both, but neither could we bear to part brother and sister.

The cats lived with us very harmoniously, taking the birth of two children in their stride and only causing the odd upset when they did outrageous or dangerous things. The usual cat stories of climbing curtains, stealing food and getting trapped in inconvenient places were the stuff of our experiences with them. When our daughter Jenny at around age four asked if we could have a dog, we laughed it off. The cats were plenty for us and I told her that I would never entertain the idea of allowing some mangy smelly pooch into our house. Dogs, I counselled her, were horrible! We had a happy two cat, one child household and in relation to this story, nothing much then happened to us until 1992, and even this event you may struggle to see the significance of, as indeed for years did I:

In June of that year I was running a four day residential workshop in a hotel in Gloucester when I was awakened in the middle of the night by an intense pain in my midriff. Assuming this was experiencing some form of potentially explosive food reaction, I went to the bathroom where it quickly became apparent that what was happening to me was nothing to do with an upset stomach. Within minutes the pain had grown to nightmare proportions and I was unable to stand up straight. I managed to get to the phone and fifteen minutes later I was in an ambulance on the way to the hospital which was mercifully close by.

A good dose of morphine later and I felt fine so I started to ask when I could leave. I had a class to run! I was a little taken aback when the consultant dealing with my case came to advise me that I wasn't taking this situation seriously enough. Did I not understand? I had acute pancreatitis, a condition that could be fatal. The only reason I felt good was because of the drugs that were now coursing through my veins. If it were not for these, I would be in immeasurable agony. Things were going to get worse and a major physical storm was coming.

It was probably the drugs, but this worried me not one bit. Sure, I was taken to a private room, had an intravenous drip in each arm, was wired to numerous machines and had blood taken every fifteen minutes, but so what? Wasn't it just part of good medical practice that the highly paid and important consultant came to see you every thirty minutes, bringing on each occasion another new colleague? Didn't every patient have three nurses ministering to them seemingly endlessly?

Two nights later my temperature had risen to 106 degrees and I was, even from my perspective, becoming quite ill. The wonderful drug induced haze had faded into near delirium and that day I had the deeply distressing experience of being visited by Sharon and Jenny. Despite her best efforts Sharon was clearly putting on a brave face and expecting the worst (I was later to learn that a doctor friend of ours had warned her that pancreatitis in its acute form was often fatal, nine out of ten times as it transpired). She had brought Jenny with her who at two years old didn't really realise what was happening, but was terribly upset when they had to go and leave me behind. The doctor's faces seemed to become progressively grimmer with each visit. Perhaps I was dying?

A few weeks before this happened I had, in pursuit of my own professional development, listened to a set of audio tapes concerning the power of mind over matter and I had been impressed with the concept. So that night, when I finally figured out that I might not make it, I decided that I would think myself better. My last cogent thought before succumbing to the delirium that was swallowing me up was that it was within my power to control what was happening to my body, and that I would survive.

Sure enough, the next morning I awoke to find my consultant in the room with six trainee doctors. Apparently my temperature had come down to a much more reasonable 103 degrees and things were looking up. I then had the bizarre experience of listening while the doctor made each of the students suggest reasons for why I was still alive. When the last one had finished without an acceptable conclusion being reached one of the students had the temerity to ask: "So why is he still alive?" In a totally matter-of-fact manner he replied: "I don't know. He should be dead."

After a few more days in hospital I was released to recuperate at home. I was immensely pleased with myself that I had managed to bring about this momentous cure but I gave no further consideration to what was behind it all. I just blandly accepted that such things were possible and that I had mastered mind over matter.

About one year later my belief system was thrown into disarray when my father contracted legionnaire's disease. After weeks in hospital with a slowly deteriorating condition he called me in to give me what could have amounted to a deathbed speech. He was very weak but still coherent and after some preliminary conversation, he asked me if I recalled the night I was 'supposed' to have died. Naturally, I did. He then explained that he wanted to tell me something about that night that I didn't know. He was aware of my proud boast that I had cured myself, but what I was unaware of was the fact that on that particular night when things were at their worst, he had called a faith healer. That man in turn had called his entire prayer group, they had done their thing and by morning, I was on the road to recovery. Now he wanted me to do the same for him.

I was in two minds over this information. For a start, it wounded my ego a little. It also contradicted what I now believed about the power of the mind vs. the power of prayer and frankly, it all sounded a bit too religious for me. Nevertheless, I did what he had asked and he made a complete recovery with alarming speed.

Rather than glibly accept his version of what 'worked' over mine, I began a cursory exploration of spiritual matters. I read a few books to gain a comparative awareness of religious belief systems but drew no conclusions.

Not too long afterwards I began travelling internationally for work and this opened up the availability of ideologies to discover and materials to study. I was struck by the realisation that the only common thread in all religions, the only belief that they all shared without exception, was an embracing of the concept of angelic beings.

I want that dog: Kaiti's tale

By 1994 I had forged a successful career as a management development specialist. I had been married to Sharon since 1987 and we now had two children. Jenny was aged four and Tristan had only just been born when I began to work all over the world, having gained the most senior learning and development position for one of the world's largest financial services institutions. The global nature of the role meant travelling a great deal and staying away for several weeks at a time. There was no routine: I could be in Hong Kong one week, the Middle East the next, then the US the week after. I lived out of anonymous hotel rooms and suitcases and I missed my family.

The glamorous appearance of the business class travel, five star hotels and exotic locations did little to compensate for the long absences. My days were distractingly busy, but evenings and weekends were full of lonely thoughts. Invitations to dine and meet the families of locals only served to magnify the feelings of separation and despite the fact that I grew personally as a result of the experience gained and the exposure to new cultures, the price was high. Increasingly I would occupy my spare time looking for presents to take back for them. On the one hand it was a method of consoling myself for their absence. On the other, it brought each one of them to the forefront of my mind and made the separation seem less real. The simple action of trying to match their likes with what I saw around me was comforting.

On one trip to the Malaysian capital Kuala Lumpur, I was staying in a hotel opposite a mall with a large Japanese department store in it. By the last day of my trip, I still hadn't found a gift for Tristan (who was still a baby at the time). Trawling the toy department for something suitable, my eye was caught by a stuffed toy dog on a high shelf at the other side of the store. As I came closer I realised that this 'dog' had clearly been designed to be cute, but that the breed did not really exist. Nonetheless, I was quite taken with it and bought it. On gifting it to Tristan it was greeted with the ambivalence of babies to most things, but it remained in his bedroom and amused me every time I saw it there. There was just something about it.

At the end of 1996 I left my employer as the overseas work and the long absences were getting to be too much. I began 1997 full of hope when I founded my own business and became self employed and things progressed well. Being my own master allowed me far more leisure time and around midyear we found ourselves at a local garden show, an indulgence to keep Sharon happy. I was waiting somewhat disinterestedly outside one of the display tents when I saw in the distance a lady walking a strange looking creature. To my immense surprise I recognised it as the living form of the peculiar toy dog I had bought for Tristan. Immediately I hurried to find Sharon to tell her what I had seen and almost dragged her and the children out of the tent. It became imperative for me to find out what this breed was and so with great excitement, I chased after the lady, my family tailing behind me. Finally I caught up and breathlessly asked what it was. She revealed that it was a Shar Pei and after fussing with it for a few minutes, I was in love.

We'd never thought of having a dog or even considered it as a vague possibility but it was only a few hours before I'd persuaded Sharon that we should get a Shar Pei. I wasn't sure why I was so attracted to the breed and it was the oddest compunction to experience. To be honest, if you'd asked me about dogs up until that point I would have claimed to hate them, describing them in the most damning of ways and being oblivious to any positive aspects that they might possess. I would characterise them as "dirty, smelly and vicious" and although I didn't really feel that way, I certainly used those adjectives to sum them up on more than one occasion.

If you're a novice in these matters, as we were, you don't even know how to find a dog as rare as a Shar Pei. Despite internet searches, we could not locate a breeder. However, we did find a dog 'broker' who, in exchange for $90, would give us a list of Shar Pei breeders with puppies. Desperate to get one as soon as possible we paid up without hesitation. The list he gave us contained only three names but sure enough, we found that there was a breeder around 120km from our house with puppies. We made a phone call and that evening Jenny and I drove over to their house.

We arrived at a pleasant country cottage that was clearly turned over to the dogs and we were led into a lounge where we experienced only our

14

second ever encounter with Shar Pei's. This time there were two of them and they were reclining on a sofa facing a television. It was on and they were watching it! In fact, they were totally transfixed by the images on the screen. If you stood in front of them blocking their view, they strained their necks to see around you. One of them even got up and moved to another chair so as to not miss anything. They paid not one bit of attention to us. The breeder did not seem to find this at all unusual and we followed her through to another room where we sat whilst she began a procession of the available puppies.

They were all gorgeous and very affectionate but I didn't feel that I 'connected' with any of them. There was the faintest trace of exasperation from the breeder as she pointed out that these were very high quality puppies, each of which was descended from a line of champions and had the potential to be a show dog. I apologised for my 'pickiness'; then with a sigh she told us that there was one more puppy. However, this was the reject of her litter. It had an overbite issue and couldn't be shown because judges would certainly reject it as a poor quality dog. It wasn't sociable. It had already developed a shy, even diffident nature. Clearly she didn't even want to show this aberration in her breed line to us, but I insisted.

Shar Pei's come in several colours: fawn was the colour of the puppies she had showed us so far; chocolate was the colour of the TV watchers; and red was the colour of the toy I had bought in Kuala Lumpur years before. When she finally brought Kaiti in, she too was red. The breeder handed her to me and unlike the others who had been lively and playful and wanting to lick me all over, this one just lay there, vaguely content to be held close but not really that bothered. I let her snuggle up to me and as she did so I experienced a sensation which at the time I dismissed as an illusion of sorts. I have already stated that I'm not prone to flights of fancy so I couldn't really accept what happened, but as I held her there it was as if something from within her, like the tendril of a plant, came out and wrapped itself around my heart. It was a creepy sensation and it would be another five years before I discovered what had actually happened. As it was, I knew instantaneously that she was the one who was going to be coming home with us. The breeder was a little surprised by the immediacy of my decision, but when I passed her to Jenny, she concurred with my choice and that was it.

15

It may seem odd to the reader that the choice of dog was made without Sharon being present. After all, bringing a new family member into your lives is a major commitment. However, somebody had to stay at home and look after Tristan and the timing was bad to have brought him along too. We had agreed it that way and Sharon was unconcerned. However, during the next week the sheer excitement of our impending arrival overcame her and we drove over again in the daytime whilst Jenny was at school with Tristan in tow. Sharon was delighted when she met the new puppy and confirmed that our choice was good. Now it was just a case of choosing a name.

The Shar Pei breed has its origins in China and is often referred to as a Chinese fighting dog, since notionally it was breed for fighting. However, if its earlier history is explored, it was actually bred for herding the Emperor's deer, hence the characteristic floppy jowls which would not damage the deer's legs if the dog tried to nip them. It is a sad history that involves near annihilation at the time of the Cultural Revolution and an unprecedented rescue mission that involved smuggling dogs into Hong Kong and thence to America where, with only fifty dogs, the breed line was recovered. In deference to her Far Eastern origins, we felt that our puppy should have a name that at least seemed to be from that part of the world. After a great deal of debate, we arrived at the name Kaiti (pronounced Katy).

Three weeks later, the whole family drove to collect Kaiti and after a very brief visit to the breeder we turned around and headed for home with our new charge on board. At the time Tristan was three and still not a fan of car journeys. He decided to cry for most of the journey back and to add to the torture of this sound, our new puppy chose to wail for her lost home. In an attempt to ease her stress we took her out of her crate and she sat on Sharon's lap where she could be cosseted. This worked until the trauma of the whole experience became too much and Kaiti was violently sick all over Sharon and the seat. We pulled into a station car park and tried to clear up some of the mess, but if a lifetime of dog ownership were to have been assessed in those opening hours, it wasn't an auspicious start.

We experienced both the excitement and trepidation of getting her home in equal measures and I can still remember vividly putting her

16

down in the enclosed back garden for the first time. She froze for a few seconds and then began to explore this strange new world. I rushed for my camera and I have the photos of those first few moments as she sniffed around the plants, the patio and assorted gardenelia. After a while, the cats put in an appearance. They were both bigger than her and it was intriguing to observe the interactions which they all took in their stride. For many hours she showed no interest in entering the house, so I stayed outside with her and barely left her side. Eventually I became tired and fell asleep flat out and face down on the lawn. Upon noticing this Kaiti came and curled up beside me. When the children approached she growled at them, clearly believing that she was on guard duty. It was to be the beginning of a lifetime of devotion.

That first night Kaiti was with us we thought we'd made the biggest mistake of our lives. We didn't really have much of an idea of what to expect but we had heard dire warnings about ensuring that the dog had its own space. We had bought a nice bed that we had placed in the kitchen and when we settled the puppy into it, she quickly fell asleep and we headed for our bed, happy to follow suit. The infernal noises began shortly after we'd dozed off and did not stop. The whole household was woken up, including Tristan who joined in with his own brand of unholy racket. We tried to settle the dog, but all to no avail, so in desperation we brought the bed upstairs and put it by my side. The noise however, did not stop and I ended up sleeping on the floor next to Kaiti. The next evening was a repeat performance, and the one after that. Then fortunately, she accepted that if I was in bed next to her that was OK. But from that point on we would never again have a dog free bedroom.

From the outset Kati has always been an unusual dog. In her youth her manner of processing whether or not she liked people involved rushing towards them with her mouth open and grasping one of their hands in her jaws. It appeared as if she was going to bite you and many visitors were quite intimidated by this approach. Of course nobody knew that she had an overbite issue and few realised in advance that her floppy jaws made the supposed 'bite' more like putting your limbs in a velvet bag. However, her advances earned her few friends, particularly as she would repeat the performance with anyone whom she hadn't seen for a while. My parents were particularly horrified when this first happened

17

and probably as a consequence, took some time to warm towards her. However, once she was sure who you were and that she liked you, Kaiti would quite literally smile when she saw you. She still does this and if I hadn't seen it with my own eyes I would not have believed it possible. It's more of a big cheesy grin and she reserves it for her most favourite people. Ironically, this included my mother who was the one most disturbed by being mouthed, and Sharon's father. His response to Kaiti's attentions was one of delight and he quickly became very fond of her. He was particularly enamoured of the fact that although months might pass between the occasions on which he saw her, she would still greet him with the same fuss and silly smile. "See, she knows me!" were the words we would hear, several times over, whenever they were reunited.

It was interesting to see how people reacted to Kaiti. To us she was stunningly beautiful but to others she was clearly ugly. As we walked her I would occasionally hear people exclaiming in horror. One day Jenny returned from walking her around the cricket green across the road from our house. She was quite upset and related the story that a man had taunted in an unpleasant tone 'you've forgotten to iron your dog." Whilst I was appalled that a grown man would upset a child in this way, I had to feel sorry for the pathetic specimen who'd probably been waiting for some while to see a Shar Pei just so that he could feel clever as a result of making this comment. Needless to say, Kaiti didn't mind one bit.

Kaiti certainly doesn't conform to most people's idea of what a pet should be and from an outsider's perspective she is very difficult to understand. It's not clear what her likes and dislikes are. She's pretty inflexible, has the most peculiar ways. She is a very fussy eater. Mood wise she alternates between complete and utter indifference and being enormously demanding of affection and attention. She is truculent, uncooperative, obstinate and downright difficult. Whilst this may not sound like a good recipe for dog ownership, we are absolutely devoted to her and despite all that is written above, she makes it obvious that she is devoted to us.

Throughout her life, she has always seemed to be able to exert a curious affect upon Sharon. If ever she is outside and wants to be let in, Sharon feels herself drawn to go to the door. Sure enough, there is Kaiti waiting.

Sharon swears she communicates about other things too, including when she wants to be fed or go for a walk. This is jokingly referred to as her 'Shar Pei mind tricks' as like Obi Wan Kenobi performing 'Jedi mind tricks' in Star Wars, she seems to be able to exert influence on others through mind control. For years I teased Sharon that only she was affected because my mind was too strong to be affected. Or maybe I just wasn't listening well enough.

Getting to grips with angels

Inexplicably in tandem with Kaiti's arrival, and more than six years after my brush with death, I rekindled my fascination with the fact that all religions had a concept of angels.

I had not really had what you would call a religious upbringing. My maternal grandfather died when I was four and my mother used to 'lend' my brother and I to my grandmother for weekends. Our presence would assuage the grief that enveloped her and give her something to look forward to. In later years she would thank my mother for this saving grace. For my brother and me it was a chance to be thoroughly spoilt for a couple of days; the only downside being that we had to go to church every Sunday. To be honest, it was so boring that it put me off organised religion completely.

So when I was due to marry into a devout Catholic family the necessity to convert to keep Sharon's parents happy was something I greeted with discomfort. Sharon herself had been involved with the 'charismatic movement' when she was at university. I didn't really 'get' this but apparently it was an outreach to people of all faiths to let them know of the joys of the Catholic experience. Although I was ambivalent with regard to her faith and even amused by the manner in which it was expressed, I was determined to get the girl. Going along with it did not seem a high price to pay and for a while at least, I did a passable job of keeping everybody happy with my conversion.

Around five years into our marriage, a deeply personal event transpired in our lives that caused both Sharon and I to withdraw from all church going activities. Privately, I was relieved.

So now, when I found myself drawn back towards what appeared to be the quasi-religious area of angels, it was somewhat of a curious step for me. As far as I was concerned, the angelic realms consisted of Archangel Gabriel who had brought news of the coming of Jesus; and Guardian Angels. And that was about it.

Nevertheless, my interest was momentarily captured and over the next few months I somewhat sceptically cross referenced a dozen serious academic tomes from as many countries and nearly as many belief systems. I found that despite changing terminologies, they all said pretty much the same thing:

- An angel is a being of pure 'Creator' light energy.
- There is what can only be termed a hierarchy of angelic beings.
- They exist in what is referred to as 'the etheric', which is most easily thought of as a parallel dimension that vibrates at a different frequency from our own (thus making it invisible to most of us), but is in the same time/space as ours.
- The role of angels is to provide general support for human endeavours with particular regard to their progress upon the 'ascension pathway'.
- They have been there since the beginning of what we conceive as time.
- Humanity has always been aware of their presence, which they have chosen to make a very open secret.
- Everybody and almost everything is on the ascension pathway.
- The term ascension pathway refers to our perpetual quest to return to that from which we come, which was referred to by various names for what we commonly refer to as God.
- Although angels are usually depicted as having a human form and a big pair of wings, they are actually beings of light that when seen, appear to have wings only because of the energy field that surrounds them.
- Our hackneyed image of them lying about on clouds and playing harps is wholly inaccurate and they actually exist in the same space as us (but in a different dimension), perpetually ready to assist us in our every endeavour, if we but reach out and ask for their help.
- Their ability to assist us is strictly regulated by a code of conduct that forbids direct intervention with our free will; but they can on occasion 'move heaven and earth' to make things happen if it is appropriate.
- On very rare occasions angels physically appear to all, but there are those who can see them all the time.

- There are many more of them than there are of us.

The details about angels seemed complex, incomprehensible and even a bit dull so I changed my focus, now gravitating towards more populist writings on the subject. What I really wanted was stories of angelic encounters, mainly to see if they reflected an experience I might have had, but not been conscious of. I read them as if they were fairy tales. There was a wealth of information about beings whom I had never come across before, yet when I heard their names, they seemed familiar to me.

I found some angel stories that were extraordinary whilst others I thought mundane and explicable through 'natural' factors. Many of the stories were of ordinary people who had no apparent agenda or reason for relating something that could make them appear as wacky as society finds UFO abductees. There was no preponderance of either male or female narratives although a vast number involved children who seemed to have a great affiliation with these unseen beings.

All this was fascinating, but like most people, I tend to believe only in what I can see. I thought that the concept of there being a bunch of beings that hung around and supported us, always unseen, was actually quite cool; but I was unable to relate anything that I read to an experience of my own. I was pretty sure I'd seen a couple of UFOs, but no big guys with energy fields, and certainly not wings.

No, it's *not* a Dalmatian: Pippa's tale

Having owned Kaiti for over a year, we began to ponder whether or not she might be lonely without another dog for company. Although Sharon was with her for the vast majority of time and she never had to spend the long days alone that are the experience of many dogs, we felt odd pangs of guilt when we read or heard information about the essential nature of dogs as being pack orientated.

After several weeks of debate, we decided that it would be the kind thing to do to get a companion for her, and immediately started the process of trying to decide what sort of dog to get. In 1998 we had begun what became an annual tradition of visiting the Crufts Dog Show, the biggest show of its kind in the world. There we had visited the 'meet the dog' section and spent a considerable time visiting all of those breeds that were of interest to us. One that had particularly caught my eye (for some reason) was a Leonberger. I had been enamoured of their huge size and gentle nature, but later when I came to put the case for one to Sharon, she had no memory of the breed. Fortunately, in pursuit of our purpose I had bought the Dorling Kindersley Dog Encyclopaedia, a richly illustrated book with a wealth of information concerning just about every breed you could think of, and then those you couldn't! However, when I showed Sharon the Leonberger picture in the book, the dog had unusual pale eyes that she found very off putting. Whilst this certainly did not match my memory of the dog that I had encountered at Crufts, it never occurred to me to look for alternative pictures on the internet and I could produce no evidence to counter her objections.

We trawled through the book at leisure and considered numerous breeds. We made short lists and tried to imagine which one would have a personality compatible with Kaiti's rather unique behaviour and attributes. But during the course of our debate, we kept coming back to the knowledge that whilst we were out on walks, Kaiti always showed a particular fondness for gun dogs. If ever we encountered one she seemed to undergo a personality transformation, becoming friendly, playful and even coquettish. It was delightful to see her behaving like an excited puppy again. With this in mind we focused our attentions around gun dogs and we were very quickly drawn to English Pointers. We particularly liked the description of their characters and there was no doubt that they were very attractive dogs. So it was eventually determined that we would get a Pointer and before we even had a dog, we decided that she would be called Pippa as the name seemed to suit the breed. I began to try and find a breeder on the internet.

After a very short period of time, I had tracked down several breeders. This included one who made it very clear on his website that he only bred dogs for sportsmen and that he had no time for people who used these working dogs as house pets as it was criminal and it shouldn't be allowed! Fortunately, I also located a new born litter on the south coast. The breeder was located very close to a location where I was due to be staying in two weeks time and although the puppies could not be taken until another two weeks after the time of my arrival, that was exactly the amount of time that I was due to stay there! We contacted the breeder and arranged that I would visit and choose a puppy the day that I arrived. The timing and the execution were perfect. It all seemed to be fated.

On the appointed day I arrived at the breeder's house which was a very well kept farm at the end of a long driveway. It seemed to be more of a hobby farm and it turned out that the husband was 'something in the city' and commuted every day whilst his wife remained at home to look after the two young children and assorted livestock. She was a very pleasant lady whose manners and solicitous behaviour suggested that she had been to a very traditional ladies college. She showed me into a kitchen that was at least twelve metres long. The lady apologised that the couple at the far end of the kitchen were people who had just chosen their puppy. Would I mind waiting at this end and keep the puppies amused while I did so? I was happy to do just that, but the puppies having been initially excited to see me, ran back to the far end of the room, jumped into a basket and promptly fell asleep. I was left sitting cross legged on the floor when one of the puppies with black and white markings got up, ran all the way back again, and deposited itself in my lap, totally at ease with me as a substitute basket.

This would have provided me with a very pleasant memory of how I came to chose our puppy, but for the fact that the breeder's little boy decided to pay me a visit. He was probably no more than three and as I was sitting on the floor, he was at my eye-level as he stood before me. He grinned manically and chattered incomprehensibly as if trying to convey some message, and then he spat in my face. Wiping the drooling mess from my nose and cheek, I good-naturedly laughed it off whilst gently explaining that spitting was not a nice thing to do. I glanced towards the mother in the hope that she had noticed and would come to my rescue but she was oblivious. Then he did it again. Not only was it very unpleasant, he also seemed to be able to produce an amazing amount of sputum. There was a little more strain in my voice as I politely asked him to stop but now he decided to turn his attention to the dog and hit the puppy who was curled up in my lap. That was too much and I said very loudly and angrily "Don't do that, it's not nice!" hoping to attract the mother's attention. She glanced my way and fortunately by this time she was just completing her transaction with the others. Having shown them out I was very relieved that she then put the boy outside.

Since the dog in my lap was the only one that was actually interested in me, it was obvious that she would be the one that I was taking home. To double up on the 'fated' feel about it, I was told by the breeder that the puppy already had a name: she was called Philippa, which of course is often abbreviated to Pippa. Again, the choice had been made without Sharon being present but this time there was no opportunity to have her check-out my selection. As it turned out, this was not a problem, but the seemingly inequitable situation would be redressed in the future.

Two weeks later I returned and was delighted to find that the child was at kindergarten. However, all of the owner's other dogs were out and about and as I was receiving my final briefing from the breeder, they milled around my car with great interest. At the time I drove a recently acquired Mercedes sports car with a grey leather interior of which I was very proud. We were just discussing whether or not the dog crate should squeeze on to the token back seat or be in the front with me when half of her pack decided that they would like to come for a drive. She was able to shoo most of them away, but a particularly handsome male called Henry took up residence in the back. Despite all coaxing, threats and attempts at bribery with biscuits, he refused to come out. I became progressively more agitated because when the breeder tried to grab his collar and pull him out, he dug his claws into the upholstery and moved backwards. Eventually I just shut the door and we walked away from the car. Immediately he wanted to get out, a fact he expressed by scratching at the door panel, which was also lined with the beautiful grey leather. When I drove away, I was traumatised, but apart from a lot of muddy paw prints, my seats had suffered no permanent damage.

English Pointers are tall, leggy noble looking creatures and even though by this time, Kaiti was fully grown, Pippa was nearly as tall as Kaiti from the moment she arrived home. Their meeting was a shock for Kaiti. Pippa was gangly, very lively and obviously used to interacting with similarly playful companions. She breezed in with all the confidence in the world and met a rather reluctant Shar Pei housemate whose real interest was in keeping her distance. The folly of our assumptions regarding Kaiti's love of gun dogs quickly became apparent. She did indeed love them. We had not been wrong in the broadest sense. It was just that her affections only extended to male gundogs. Rather than form the firm friendship we had hoped for, Pippa quickly became the bane of Kaiti's existence and from that point onwards, Kaiti never got a moment of peace.

It was not Pippa's fault as she was most certainly only doing that which came naturally to her; but when she arrived with us she was at the stage of play biting, tearing around madly and wanting to wrestle. Kaiti on the other hand had never done any these things, perhaps because she had arrived in a household where she was the only dog. Now the younger dog was most insistent that her elder colleague behave as she did. For her part, Kaiti treated Pippa with disdain; but the assault of the puppy upon her life was unassailable. Within days her coat bore the scars of the numerous puncture wounds inflicted by rapidly growing teeth, and my treasured dog had become a substitute chew toy. I was mortified and assumed the role of Kaiti's defender. It became quite difficult for me to accept Pippa's behaviour and it was only Kaiti's tolerant and apparently more accepting approach that saved me from being completely put off our new dog. For a while, it was really touch and go.

As the weeks passed things got a little better and Pippa could be taken out for walks. I have a particularly vivid recollection of taking her for her first outing. Rather than walk in the local urban area I decided that an experience of the countryside would be preferable; so we made the fifteen minute journey from our home to an expansive wooded area nearby. Upon arrival I let the dogs out and Kaiti went dashing off madly as she usually did with this kind of release. Pippa however was paralysed with fear. Her confidence totally deserted her and she remained rooted to the spot, trembling uncontrollably. The only cause was the unfamiliarity of the surroundings, yet she remained there for fifteen minutes before, in total frustration, I walked away. Tentatively, she followed for a little way, then raced back to the car where she cowered. I gave up and we went home. The next day I tried again and it was as if a different dog had come with me. This time she clearly relished the experience and galloped around with the sheer joy of a racehorse at pasture. Pippa's pleasure with the freedom of running free was evident, and in those youthful days she could run like the wind. Thereafter in the woods, we seldom walked her on a leash and she would race around excitedly, covering huge distances and going far off into the distance until she was only a spot on the horizon. At a single call she would return at great speed and obediently stay with us until she was released again.

In the house, we began to notice how much Pippa craved affection. Despite her rapidly growing size she seemed to view herself as a lap dog and loved nothing better than to cuddle up with me when I was sitting in my recliner. Although her sheer size made this an uncomfortable impossibility after a short while, her need for attention grew and grew. If she was not being stroked by a human, she would move her body backwards and forwards underneath a large architectural plant in our lounge so that the touch of the leaves simulated the physical contact of stroking. Her need for physical contact is something that has never left her and there is a guarantee in our household that if ever another dog is receiving any attention, Pippa will appear and position herself between the person stroking and the other dog so that you cannot ignore her. In fact it is a very bad idea for strangers to pay her any attention because if they do, she will never leave them alone.

Over the coming months Pippa developed into a stunning creature. If we had been possessed of any interest in showing her, we are convinced that she could have been a show winning champion. She has always been a dog of tremendous grace and beauty and despite her initial responses to Kaiti, she is a very gentle dog. This softness seemed to be apparent to all-comers and when we encountered other people whilst out and about, invariably they would stop to pet her. She responded with nuzzling guaranteed to delight the crowd and she held a particular magnetism for children. Invariably upon seeing her they would squeal in delight: "Oh look, it's a Dalmatian" and race over to be with her. We lost count of the number of times that we felt obliged to correct this error, pointing out with mild irritation that she was actually an English Pointer. Eventually we gave up, allowing them to believe their self deception that they might indeed have encountered a cast member of the live action version of 101 Dalmatians.

She may have made it as a movie star, but she would undoubtedly have made the most appalling gundog if natural talent is anything to go by. Pointers are trained not to fear gunshots and literally 'point' to downed game birds in the field. They freeze motionless, raise a front paw underneath them, hold their tails outstretched behind them and their noses forward to direct their masters to follow their line to the prey. They are supposed to do this instinctively. Pippa did once do a 'full' point just like this. It was awesome to see but she was pointing at a housefly on a window!

For a brief period we had a quasi tradition that once a year we would make a family visit to the beach on a hot summer's day. We actually lived three hours away from the nearest coast and would set off in mid afternoon, ensuring our arrival as everyone else was leaving. The beach was a long and sweeping expanse which we would almost have to ourselves, and Pippa and Kaiti could be let off their leashes to run freely. I have the happiest memories of watching their unfettered excitement as they raced crazily around the sands, chasing seagulls and splashing in the shallows. On one occasion Pippa spotted a young child in the distance and full of love for the whole world raced towards it at breakneck speed. She is a supremely gentle creature but from the child's perspective making that approach she must have been terrifying. I can still hear the squeals of anguish he let out, causing Pippa to stop in her tracks and return at an equally fast pace, tail firmly between her legs. The visits were rounded off with that great British tradition of fish and chips served in newspapers and I was never quite sure which the dogs enjoyed most: the running on the beach or their share of the supper.

To this day, despite old age and the onset of rheumatism, Pippa's love of running free has never left her. It is very sad for us to see how exertion can leave her stiff and tired but fortunately the healing effects of a magnetic collar prevent her from suffering. She is still a great companion on a hike and you can still guarantee that if you walk 10km, Pippa will do 20km. Over the years she has assumed the position of alpha female and behaves as if she were nobility within our house. I think of her more as a Grand Duchess since, as far as I'm concerned, Kaiti will always be the Queen.

An angelic encounter?

You may recall that my motivation for leaving full time employment had been to spend more time at home and avoid the international travel that had become the all pervasive feature of my life. However, throughout Kaiti and Pippa's puppy years I was away for a great deal of the time due to the fact that after the publication of my book on leadership, demand for my services rose and I ended up spending even more time overseas than I had done whilst an employee. Psychologically this was a better place to be in because at least in doing this I was serving my own interests and reaping the rewards. I would go from country to country without returning home, often on a round-the-world ticket and stayed in some amazing hotels. I could easily write another book about the many awesome experiences I had on my travels, but perhaps the most notable one occurred in 2001 when I found myself working in Sedona, Arizona.

Since 2000 I had spent a substantial amount of time delivering development programs in Sedona for a large US client. Sedona has a unique energy and I loved the awesome landscape with its red rocks and sense of mystery. The classes left me with free weekends, so I travelled the area extensively and became quite a well known figure locally.

One Sunday morning in February one of my team and I decided to drive to Flagstaff, about 50 kilometres away. We drove north, climbing through a beautiful river valley and increasingly heavy snow. We ploughed on, confident in the Ford Excursion I was driving, a massive long wheel base SUV.

Returning, we wound downhill round a series of right angled bends and hairpin turns. The road became progressively steeper until at one point a cliff wall stretched high up on the roadside nearest to us; whilst on the other side the road dropped away alarmingly. Ahead of us was a sedan obviously lacking in four wheel drive and as a consequence, the driver was taking things very cautiously. We could just about make out the occupants as an elderly couple, apparently out for a leisurely drive and clearly enjoying the scenery. Throughout, I had been maintaining a cautious distance but I was shocked when suddenly and without an observable reason the elderly driver braked hard. We were aghast to see that they were stopping to take a picture!

I began to brake but our outrageously heavy vehicle, at such a steep gradient and in snow, barely slowed. I braked harder but instead of creating the affect I desired, we began to slide. Those in front showed no sign of awareness of what was behind them, nor did they move on. Impact was seconds away so to avoid smashing into the old folks, I plotted a route that might just take us between their car and the cliff face and steered accordingly. Then at the last moment, their car moved off. But it was too late for us to change our course; the wheels were already trapped within deep snow. As Ed and I braced ourselves for impact, the Ford suddenly lurched over on the passenger side at a 45 degree angle and stopped – literally - 3 inches from the rock face.

It took us a few seconds to realize that the road was separated from the cliff by a deep snow filled ditch into which we had now careened. It was this that had prevented the course correction and this that now held our vehicle captive. We were well and truly wedged in it. Leaning over at this crazy angle, we both reached for mobile phones only to find that there was no signal. We struggled to haul ourselves up and out, forced by the angle at which we were listing to use the glove box as a step, and jumped down onto the road. The elderly couple drove on, seemingly oblivious or careless as to our fate.

Behind us cars stopped, unwilling to pass since this would require them to steer near to the cliff edge on the opposite side of the road. As I looked at them imploringly, they watched impassively, waiting to see what would happen. The minutes that passed seemed like hours as we struggled to think of what to do next. All I could think of was the fact the new group that we were due to train was due to arrive in a few hours time and I was supposed to be there to greet them. Time passed and panic began to set in. There was no way to move the gargantuan beast without heavy lifting gear, no way to call for help and not so much as a word of sympathy from our fellow road users.

And then for some reason, perhaps out of desperation, it occurred to me that if angels were real, now would be a very good time for one to make an appearance.

I turned to see, further up the road, a bright red Chevy Blazer come into view. I noticed absent mindedly that it was spotlessly clean when all the other vehicles were coated in the dirty snow thrown up by their car wheels. Fearlessly braving the cliff edge, the driver pulled the Blazer up alongside us. "Need a hand?" said the driver and without so much as another word he pulled in front of us and began to unwind the winch attached to the rear of his SUV. He made no eye contact and he barely threw me a glance as I watched him. It would later strike me as strange that for one who is normally so observant, I could recall none of his features.

I was immediately excited about the prospect of rescue but Ed was quick to manage my expectations: "Don't get your hopes up. We're wedged in good and tight." he said in a low voice: "The Blazer is way too small to do this. It only weighs a couple of tons at most and our truck weighs over four and a half tons. And take a look at the size of the winch he's using. It needs some kind of power lift to get this thing out not something you drag logs with. The winch will just burn out with the strain and he's going to end up damaging his nice new truck. This isn't going to happen. No way!"

The owner of the Blazer obviously shared none of Ed's concerns. He quickly hooked up the cable and fired up his engine. My enthusiasm was dampened by Ed's words and feeling somewhat crestfallen, I watched with zero expectation whilst Ed was just embarrassed for the guy. Then to our immense shock the Excursion leapt effortlessly from the ditch in one go. Ed was speechless. I almost went into shock. Our vehicle had not so much as one scratch on in. The Blazer guy was already uncoupling the tow line and without a word he turned and hurried back towards his car. The whole extraction had taken less than a minute.

Coming to my senses I ran after him, calling heartfelt thanks but he just waved and drove off. I raced back to our SUV, anxious to unblock the road and sped off as fast as conditions permitted. Through the descending bends we caught sight of the Blazer ahead of us and I accelerated, possessed with a strange urge to follow. We began to gain on him and by the time we reached the bottom of the valley, we were no more than 200 metres behind. Ahead, the Blazer turned a bend that was almost 180 degrees, and as it did so, it passed briefly out of sight.

But we were soon round the bend too, turning onto the long straight road that lay ahead. You could probably see for nearly a mile. There were no side roads, no turn offs and no lay-bys. But the bright red Blazer had vanished.

We sat in silence, both wearing the same puzzled expression on our faces. Finally after a full five minutes had passed it was Ed who broke the silence. "So where do you think that guy went then?" I paused for thought but all I could say was: "Let's not talk about it". And we didn't.

I have often reflected upon the impossibility of the event and the roles played by everyone. I have even wondered if time has caused me to distort what happened. For a long while, it was only Ed's concurrence with my account – or his even more miraculous version of it – that convinced me that I didn't imagine it all. I now accept that what happened was predestined and everybody did what they were supposed to do that day so that sometime thereafter, I would have absolute belief that there are angels. But at this point I was still many years away from reaching this conclusion. In fact, it was a couple of years before I even entertained the idea of there being angels again.

Houdini on four legs: Emily's tale

With the increased travel the strain on family life returned and now I also had the added dimension of missing the dogs to contend with. To cope with the frequent absences I would fly Sharon and the children to wherever I was working whenever I could. Consequently they began to see a great deal of the world and in one year alone, Jenny (who was by now eleven) got to visit the Far East, the Middle East, the United States and eight different European countries. In fact she had seen more of the world by the time she was this age than I had by the time I was thirty five.

It resulted in some great holidays for us as I would tag these visits on to the end of business trips, but for the two dogs that waited for us at home, it meant frequent visits to kennels. They never seemed to reproach us for our absence upon our return, but Pippa would become very stressed as she was led to her prison cell at the boarding kennels. Kaiti on the other hand displayed stoicism and bravely strode into the cage. On our return they would both be equally ecstatic and Kaiti's manic grin would be visible for a long time after she got home.

When I was away on my own, my returns were heralded by excited barking on Pippa's part and a seeming desire from Kaiti to eat me when I arrived. Sharon and the kids quickly learned that it was easier to let the dogs be the ones to greet me first since they would only be shoved aside by a large Pointer and a Shar Pei in rapture. On one occasion I lay on the floor in the hallway shortly after I got in and Kaiti completely smothered my mouth with her jowls. The only thing that prevented it from being a full on kiss was the absence of her tongue in my mouth, but this was only because my mouth was closed, not because she wasn't trying.

After four years of being an absentee husband, father and dog master things started to get to be too much. I was due to leave on yet another round-the-world trip that would take me away for three months when I suddenly realised that I desperately didn't want to leave. In the run up to all trips I would always get to a point where I became morose and emotional. But this was different. I can best describe it as an emotional meltdown and it was a combination of feelings of loss, grief, guilt and all-pervasive sadness mixed together. In the agony of having to go away again I vowed that this would be my last long trip. And it was. I began to centre my business upon Europe and limit my expeditions to a duration of two weeks only. My peace of mind and our family life was rapidly restored.

Perhaps because things became more settled, or perhaps because three years passed since we had bought Pippa, Sharon got the itch to have a smaller dog. She had always been drawn to smaller breeds and it had been at my insistence that we ended up with a mid-size and a large dog. Another visit to Crufts rekindled our excitement with the vast variety of personalities and temperaments that were out there in the dog world. We developed a strange logic: if owners enjoyed the experience of sharing their lives with their dogs, and due to their longevity, across the course of a lifetime the average owner had the experience of owning only three dogs, what other pleasures did they deprive themselves of? We certainly loved being with our dogs. So did we really want to deprive ourselves? The answer was of course "no".

We began perusing our Dorling Kindersley dog encyclopaedia again but I was unhappy with the idea of having a lap dog sized creature around. Then Sharon came across a breed that was previously unknown to us: the Basset Griffon Vendeen or BGV for short. They were originally bred for hunting game in France and there were actually two varieties: the Grand Basset that was used for hunting game as large as wild boar; and the Petit Basset that were particularly expert at catching hares. The breed was relatively rare (the Grands in particular being almost unknown in North America) and we had certainly never seen one unless we had passed them by without noticing at Crufts. I liked the look of the Grands but it was the Petits that caught Sharon's attention. The long, low bodied hairy dogs pictured had a roguish look in their eyes that was totally reflective of their mischievous temperament, as we would soon discover. They were just small enough for Sharon to count them as small dogs and not so small that I would find them unacceptable.

After some further research we located a breeder who lived surprisingly near to us and we arranged to pay her a visit. A few days later we arrived at Clipperdown Cottage and we were welcomed by Viv Phillips, the breeder. Unbeknownst to us at the time, our meeting with her was

38

to prove one of the most enduring relationships we have had with a breeder. Viv is one of those people who is fiercely protective of her dogs and definitely prefers them to most people. When you first meet her, she's sizing you up to see whether or not you'll make a good owner for her dogs and it can make her appear a little stand-offish. Once you get past the tough exterior there's a heart of gold there, but never mistake the fact that the dogs are her priority.

After we had known Viv for some years, her home was broken in to and several of her dogs were stolen, including one that was pregnant. This awful phenomenon was an increasing one in the UK; but whereas most owners will accept the tragedy and get on with their lives, there was no way that Viv would ever have accepted that anybody would get away with stealing her dogs. Her palpable distress and heartache was channelled into a furious desire to get them back and within days she had organised national coverage of her story which included newspaper, radio and television coverage. The missing animals became recognisable public figures and faced with the pressure of such publicity, the thieves had no choice but to surrender the dogs.

On this first meeting she showed us both Petits and Grands. On contact I still favoured the larger BGVs, but as I had it all my own way with Pippa, I had to give in to Sharon's choice. Whilst at this point there were no puppies, some were expected and we put our names on a waiting list. We were a little concerned that Viv seemed so indifferent to meeting us but we brushed the thought aside.

A few months later Viv got in touch to let us know that puppies had been born. When we returned to Clipperdown Cottage, it was almost like meeting a different person. She explained that she had so many time wasters who never pursued their initial interest that she always waited until the second occasion of meeting them before she 'put out' and since we were here again, we were OK!

We were taken back to the kennels and shown a litter of Petit Bassets that were around three weeks old. The mother was not there but Viv was very keen that we should meet her to see her temperament and assured us that she was somewhere around. She called her by name, but no dog appeared. She called again and still no dog. Then she positively hollered and around the door of a kennel a few doors down, a head appeared. This was the missing mother and Viv encouraged her to come and visit with us. The dog slowly ambled out of the kennel and walked off in the opposite direction, its nose pinned to the ground. Viv called again and it cast a dismissive glance our way before returning to the scent it was apparently so interested in. Finally Viv went and fetched her and we met our future puppy's mother. I should have known right there and then what we were getting ourselves in to. The signs were on the wall. If this was what the mother was like, how would the puppy be?

Pretty much exactly the same as it turned out. From the moment we collected Emily in August she was a real chip off the old block. Of all of the dogs that we own, Emily is the least biddable. Occasionally she will sit when asked but only if the food incentive is powerful enough. But as for any of the stay or come stuff, forget it! Thus far she is the only one of our dogs who has gone through two separate sets of puppy training classes, and each of these has been to no avail.

Sharon has vivid memories of taking Emily to her second set of classes which were held in the outdoors. The training took place amidst the peaceful setting of a local park and it was a real pleasure for the participants to put their dogs through their paces in the freshness of the spring days. At least it was for all of those who weren't called Sharon. After a few weeks, and on an unfortunately wet and rainy day, the class began off-the-leash work. One by one, the participants unfettered their pets to practice their recalls and distance commands. Despite Sharon's protests that if she were let off, Emily might not come back, the instructor confidently insisted that our dog also be freed to show what she could do. And she did. Emily promptly ran away and could be seen and heard in the distance noisily trying to capture what might have been an elusive rabbit or simply a dragonfly. By the time the next class arrived for their session, Sharon had been trying to get Emily back for half an hour and her frantic calls interrupted most of the next class. After that she was too embarrassed to go back again.

To this day Emily is the most wilful, disobedient and independent minded of all of our dogs. She is one of those dogs best described as 'a character'. I have personally spent more hours looking for a missing and unresponsive Emily than all of our other dogs put together. She's also

40

very cute, loving and great fun and immediately looked to Pippa as a surrogate mother.

At least the two of them were happy together, but even owning (what appeared to many) an outrageous three dogs, all of whom lived in our house, we still had no clue as to what was actually going on and what lay ahead.

Voices in my head

Having Emily with us was like having an angel in the house: a fallen one! Her antics kept Sharon and I on our toes and disrupted the trouble free relationship that Pippa and Kaiti had fallen into, which basically consisted of them ignoring one another. Emily however, could not be ignored and insisted on muscling in on everything that went on in the house.

I have since speculated that perhaps it was the proximity of this loveable 'little devil' that caused the idea of angels to once more resurface in my consciousness.

Ironically, my apparent encounter on the road from Flagstaff had actually marked a cessation of interest. I read no more books and thought no more about them. I 'dined out' on the story many times, always ending with the cliff-hanger line "So *what* do you think the Blazer driver was then?" and offering no explanation of my own. These were the only occasions on which angels filtered into my thoughts and I became more interested in First Nations culture and history.

Seemingly by chance I met up with an ex colleague. We agreed to have lunch and after the usual mundane discussions of who'd done what, she revealed to me that she had experienced a telephone session of something called 'channelling' with a lady in America. Apparently this woman was some kind of go between who was able to transmit messages from the angelic realms into our own. My friend had talked with her for an hour and received guidance that she found inspiring and nurturing. The channel had spoken in another voice and seemed to assume wisdom beyond that which she could have known as a human being. Despite my copious reading, I had no recollection of ever hearing of this before. I knew quite well what a medium was (and I'd even been to see the world famous medium and author Doris Stokes on stage twenty years previously) but I hadn't realised you could actually talk to angels.

That night as I relayed the tale to Sharon, I was careful to inject the right amount of semi-mocking tone into my voice; I didn't want her to think I actually believed in the reality of my colleague's experience. In her Catholic charismatic days at University I knew that she had been involved with people who had 'spoken in tongues', which I imagined might be something similar; but I was still conscious of the fact that she might decry this as some kind of heresy. Quite contrary to my expectations she seemed to find the whole story riveting and asked many questions. What then followed was a verbal dance around one another, each trying to discover precisely how credible the other found the idea of channelling and how interested the other was in actually experiencing it. It didn't take too long to become clear that both of us found it fascinating and both of us would like to have a session with the woman my friend had been in touch with. Perhaps this could be as exciting as some of those 'fairy stories' I'd read a few years back!

The very next day we got on the internet and arranged a convenient time for a session with the lady and paid in advance for a one hour channelling. In the email exchanges that followed we were told that we could pretty much ask anything that we liked with the exception of questions that involved predictions for our future. It was also recommended that we plan our questions in advance since the experience might have the potential to leave us tongue-tied.

About two weeks later at the appointed hour we put in our transatlantic call and a friendly voice welcomed us and explained what would happen. Then after a few moments pause, her voice changed slightly and we were speaking to an angel. Over the course of the next sixty minutes we asked questions on a wide variety of subjects that affected our lives. The experience was revealing, supportive and helpful. It was all very matter of fact and when it was over, we simply thanked the lady who had now returned to being herself and hung up.

The conversations about that call went on for months. In hindsight I find it odd that we questioned not one single aspect of the veracity of the messages we were given. We had no doubt at all that the experience was genuine. But apart from the friend who had led us to this lady in the first place, we told nobody about our session.

Then, seemingly by chance once again, I met up with an ex boss. I had not seen him for twenty five years and we arranged to meet for lunch. I

44

had always admired this individual as he was a very down to earth sort of person, in actual fact an accountant, so perhaps that was to be expected! We had lot of catching up to do and the conversation flowed easily. Then after about an hour and with no warning that something strange was coming, he told me that he and his wife were deeply into 'new age' matters. They were both involved with a particular new age teacher whose name I recognised due to owning a copy of one of his books. The author was big into angels. I was initially a little incredulous that my friend, who in many ways was so 'ordinary', could now be relating these extraordinary things to me. I hid my surprise well, privately thinking him quite brave to allow me to be privy to such personal information. If I held these kinds of beliefs, I certainly wouldn't be so forthcoming in admitting it! So as to make him feel that I was empathetic to what he was sharing I began to reveal some of my own experiences that could be described as broadly spiritual in nature. We swapped a few stories and then I told him about the channelling we had paid for, believing that the strangeness of it all would level the playing field between us. But in my friend's eyes it seemed a totally normal thing to have done. He regularly attended channelling sessions with an Archangel called Michael.

A few bells started to ring at this time because the lady we'd had the session with also channelled a 'Michael', although she hadn't said that it was *Archangel* Michael. I was interested by some of the synchronicities between our lives, particularly the element of searching for spiritual meaning. After a pleasant few hours we parted and whilst walking to the Underground in London, I rang Sharon to relay my experience. However, she was too caught up in her own discoveries: while I had been away, and at almost precisely the time that I had been discussing these matters with my friend, she had been mulling over our channelling and had found herself on the internet. Once there she discovered the website of a lady called Ronna Herman who channelled an Archangel called Michael! Sharon was very excited as messages intended for all were displayed on the website and she couldn't wait for me to get home to see them.

Curiously, when I got home a few hours later, I was totally unengaged by the site. I didn't want to read the messages and I didn't feel drawn to it in any way. Sharon was disappointed and tried to persuade me to get into it, but I would have none of it. It was a few days later I noticed that the site was saved on my internet favourites list so I highlighted the name so as to delete it. By accident the site was called up again and just as I was about to close it, I happened to notice a tab which indicated that Ronna ran seminars. I guess it was the professional presenter in me that wanted to know more, but whatever the reason, I went to have a look. I had the impression that the content was vague, intangible and certainly incomprehensible to me. So I was more than a little surprised at myself that within half an hour, I had signed up to go to a two day event in Rotterdam. It was a mere three weeks away. I didn't know why I was going; I didn't know what I would discover; I didn't even really want to go.

Nevertheless, go I did. On the day it began I found myself the only Brit in a room with over two hundred other Europeans, feeling like a fish out of water. A lot of them seemed to know each other and the material presented by Ronna seemed second nature to them. To me it was somewhat esoteric and rather mysterious but I found that I understood most of it. I took some notes and found the concepts fascinating. The fact that it was in English was a big plus, but I didn't interact with my fellow attendees. They were without doubt a very pleasant and accepting group, tolerant of a fellow European who only spoke one language when they all spoke at least two or three. But by my down to earth standards some seemed to be a little off the wall. Worse still, some were prone to toe curlingly embarrassing moments of emotional expression which, to a stiff upper lipped Brit, were just too much.

On the last day our host announced that we would be doing something called an 'activation meditation'. Apparently this would involve some kind of guided meditation that would enable us to channel angels for ourselves. I was more than a little incredulous that this was possible; but since I was there and I'd paid for it, I'd try anything once! When we began I felt a little self-conscious at being told to close our eyes. I peeped at those around me and they all seemed to be taking it perfectly seriously so I towed the line and followed suit. The experience of being guided by the visual imagery that her words suggested was certainly an enjoyable one. It went on for maybe twenty minutes and it was very peaceful and relaxing. Ultimately though, I was left with a feeling of disappointment: when we were 'brought back' from the meditation, nothing had changed and the activation, for me at least, had failed.

The weekend ended with Ronna giving a lengthy message channelled from Archangel Michael. It was very impressive, very interesting and certainly a highlight of the weekend. I would have plenty to tell Sharon about when I got home.

It transpired that Sharon had a feeling that something 'big' would result from me going to this seminar, although she couldn't define what. I was able to relate the learning points from my two and a half pages of notes but she was equally disappointed that there was no tangible result. I think she hoped that I would change as a result of it and become more angelic myself. No such luck! So passing the event off as merely an interesting experience, our lives returned to our normal routine of looking after three dogs, two cats and two kids. And life may well have stayed in this comfortably normalcy had it not been for the fact that five months later, whilst sitting talking to Sharon at our kitchen table, a voice in my head that was unrecognisable as my own, said "May I?" Apparently my head dropped to my chest and the next thing I knew was that Sharon was staring at me with an awed expression. For the last five minutes I had been speaking with someone else's voice.

A cry for help: Dougal's tale

As you might imagine, suddenly speaking with someone else's voice can be a disturbing event but in actual fact my initial reaction was one of ambivalence. In part I was fascinated that this had happened. On the other hand I was somewhat concerned over its implications, particularly in terms of the way other people might regard us if they knew.

Those who were aware that we had three dogs already seemed to consider our lives a little bizarre. If I had added to this knowledge the fact that some kind of entity had used my body to speak through, I can just imagine what the response would have been. They would have waited for my head to start spinning around and green stuff to come out of my mouth.

So it was something of a relief when the next day we got a distracting email from Viv Phillips, the breeder who'd sold Emily to us. We'd kept in touch periodically to give her updates about Emily and followed her progress in the doggie world. She had a great number of champion show dogs and that past weekend we had been to Crufts to see her compete. She had won several titles to add to the dog's already massive collection.

However, the email told a less happy story. Viv explained that four years previously she'd sold a Grand Basset Griffon Vendeen and a Petit Basset Griffon Vendeen to a man who was interested in showing them. He'd had some success with the Grand who'd won best in show in the puppy class at another major dog show. However, he'd then got bored with the dogs and decided to breed Rottweilers instead. Consequently the BGVs had been left languishing in their pen in the garden for two years, unkempt and with little attention being paid to them.

Shortly before Crufts Viv had got wind of this and was livid to imagine animals that she had bred and still cared about a great deal could be treated in this way. As Emily's tale suggests, she's not the sort of lady to take this sort of thing lying down and so when the opportunity presented itself, she furiously confronted the owner at Crufts, creating something of a scene. Perhaps to avoid further embarrassment the man agreed to return the dogs and true to his words they were brought to Viv's house the next day. It was clear that they had just been groomed and that maybe the owner was trying to hide some shame in his treatment of them. But he still didn't have the nerve to face Viv again. They were delivered by courier, and unceremoniously deposited on her doorstep.

In immediate response, Viv sent out the email as a plea to all her known and trusted BGV owning friends to ask if anyone could rescue this pair. It was the first occasion on which we'd come across anything like this. We had seen the press campaigns at Christmas and bumper stickers that said "A dog is for life, not just for Christmas" but they didn't really have any meaning for us. We couldn't conceive that once someone had taken on the responsibility for a pet in their lives that they'd ever want to get rid of it. But here we were, faced with first hand evidence of it. We were quite moved and without giving it any further thought, we offered to come over to see the dogs, just to get to know them and thereafter, from a position of knowledge, see if we could think of anyone who might want them.

When we arrived Viv led us to a spacious pen in her back garden where the two were being kept. The Grand Basset, who was a gorgeous mostly white male called Dougal immediately stood up against the bars and licked me, almost as if he recognised me. In that moment I knew that we weren't going to be recommending him to anyone and it was as if Sharon had the same knowing simultaneously.

Viv encouraged us to take them for a walk on our own and as we walked we discussed whether or not it would be practical to have a fourth dog. Since our garden was so small and the house wasn't exactly huge, we were already bursting at the seams. Nevertheless, our discussion of the practicalities went something along the lines of Sharon saying: "Do you think we could manage another dog?" Me saying: "Yes" And Sharon saying "Alright then, which one should we take?" Sharon greatly favoured the Petit Basset who was called Haggis. She already doted on Emily and so getting another PBGV seemed like the obvious thing to do. She also thought that Dougal was too big (although he was considerably smaller than Pippa) and found that he pulled too much to walk him with any ease. But Dougal was the obvious choice for me: I couldn't cope with another potentially mad runaway PBGV, but more importantly, I felt that Dougal was meant to come with us. And what's more, I felt he knew this too.

I relayed my feeling to Sharon who accepted it totally and come with us he did.

When we got him home he was beside himself with excitement and was wildly affectionate. He greeted the females with impeccable manners and they welcomed him in return. He enjoyed exploring the garden but was afraid to come inside and although we could lure him just inside the door, he would quickly turn and run out again. The likely origins of this behaviour became clear at one point when having got him a metre indoors, Sharon raised her arm to get something from a cupboard and he cowered with the obvious expectation of being hit, then fled. Happily, by evening he felt confident enough to come all the way into the kitchen, and once he had made it into the hallway, that was it, there were no holds barred! That night he slept in our bedroom at Sharon's side and has done so ever since.

Over the coming weeks as we came to know him more, other experiences from his past life began to surface. The most disturbing amongst these was his terror of black dogs. I believe his previous owner had taunted him with the Rottweilers, although this is only my suspicion. Whatever the reason, the reaction was palpable and I'm not sure that he ever got over this. Fortunately, he never sees black dogs these days.

A slightly heartbreaking feature of owning Dougal was that if ever we went on holiday he would pine for us and apparently go into depression. We would return from a fortnight's holiday to hear reports that he had spent the time in the kennel hardly moving. Upon being freed, he would greet us with great enthusiasm but alarmingly, he had lost the ability to wag his tail, having not once shown pleasure with it whilst we were away. It would take a few days for the wag to return and a week before he could thrash the floor with pleasure, his trademark if his name is so much as mentioned.

Despite all of this, he settled with us and our growing pack almost instantaneously. In the five years that he has now been with us he has proved to be a wonderful and loving animal who now seems to have forgotten most of his past experiences and is blessed with a healthy love of all of the pleasures life has to offer. Of all of the dogs, it was Dougal who always seemed to be the keenest to accompany us wherever we went. Even if it meant being left in the car for a couple of hours while we did shopping, he would still want to make the journey. Feeling sorry for him we would often take him out and walk him around towns with us. Sharon would go inside the stores and I would stand outside with Dougal waiting patiently by my side.

We allowed Dougal to be omnipresent partly because, unlike the other dogs, he so desperately wanted to come; but it was also because we observed that he had a curious affect on other people that was instantaneous and magnetic. As soon as Dougal appeared, people would come and talk to us. We would find ourselves approached by total strangers who doubtless under any other circumstances would have passed us by without a second glance. It was as if there was something about his energy that drew others to him and as they petted and fussed with him, we got used to hearing people remark that he looked like an angel. One day a lady actually crossed the street and stood before him with a look of pure shock on her face. She put her fingers to her lower lip and gasped. "Did you know he's an angel?"

Learning to channel

Although he was a wonderful distraction for me, for Sharon, Dougal seemed to be a reminder of what the voice that spoke through me had imparted to her. Despite my best attempts to be evasive about the issue, she now assumed the role of my conscience and regularly brought to my attention what had been said.

Whoever had been using my body had relayed to Sharon that it was an experiment to see if I was capable of being utilised in this way since, having volunteered, 'they' would like to take me up on my offer. My volunteering had apparently taken place at the time of the conference in Rotterdam via the activation meditation, but the origins of my capacity to be used in this way appeared to go back to my teenage years. As it turned out, it was a lot further than that.

The voice had requested that I learn to develop the ability to be a channel and for this purpose, there were already four 'guides' who were waiting just to assist with this task. All I had to do was get myself into a meditative state and listen for their voices. So with a modicum of reluctance, I began to pursue this end.

When people learn to meditate the greatest skill that they acquire is the ability, at will, to quiet their minds. We are so full of the incessant chatter of our consciousness that we are seldom able to hear what else is available to us if we could but listen. Unfortunately for me I had never learned this technique, yet the voice had explained to Sharon that I must acquire the skill before any progress could be made.

Curiously, a flyer arrived as part of the usual junk mail that extolled the virtues of a CD of meditation music. Notionally it was meant to transport you to an altered state of awareness without having to learn any particular technique. That sounded like just the job to me, so I ordered it immediately and within the week it arrived. Thereafter, I would sit in my home-based office for half an hour or an hour listening to it with my eyes closed, desperately trying to get myself to shut up!

Weeks went by and no voice came back. My ability to quiet my mind was severely lacking and as the time passed, with each new session I began to think there was actually more going on than less. Then just when I was beginning to imagine that the whole exercise was futile and had resolved that I would give up, I heard something that sounded like I was being spoken to from a great distance. The voice was very indistinct but I was pretty sure that it wasn't me that I'd heard. So day after day, I continued to immerse myself in the music and hope that in the not-so-empty silence of my mind, the voice might return. Sure enough, after another month it did. Then on a daily basis what I was hearing became clearer and the indistinct words became comprehensible sentences and what the sentences revealed was mind-blowing.

It quickly became apparent that I was actually speaking to the four promised beings who introduced themselves by name. Although they spoke with a single voice, I was somehow aware of their differences and soon their sound was accompanied by a visual image, seen with my eyes closed, of them standing around me. Each had a particular purpose in being present which they also explained at length. It felt like we had become intimately acquainted since they knew everything about me although I knew nothing of them. Minute long conversations became twenty minute explanations of that which I needed to know.

As you might imagine, suddenly finding that you can talk to angels personally felt a bit like being given the keys to the universe. Over time, as my listening skills and their clarity improved, I was able to ask a whole host of questions the answers to which would form a book in itself. For the purposes of this story there are certain essential pieces of information that need to be explained, which I think of as the basics of the understanding that they imparted.

What are humans?

Like angels, we too are beings of light. However, we have elected to undergo a physical occurrence of life in what are referred to as the third dimensional realms. We incarnate with a density of being that allows us to go through a completely different set of experiences from those of the angels, who are there to look after us to the extent to which they are able.

Why are we here?

We are here to gain experience and to learn. Across a number of lifetimes our learning criteria changes and develops as we make progress through what are called soul levels.

What happens to us after we die?

After death we transition to what may be thought of as another dimension where we review our state of learning and plan and prepare for our next life. When the planning is complete, we return. In earthly terms, this is usually after a period of not less than six months. In terms of the dimension to which we have transitioned, it is the equivalent of many years.

How many lifetimes do we have?

As many lifetimes as we need to achieve the learning that is our goal. There is no limitation and a single learning point that escapes an individual may need to be re-experienced many times over.

What are soul levels?

Soul levels may be understood in the same way that we understand our lives: We begin as babies and transition into childhood, adulthood and finally old age.

Baby soul lifetimes are spent getting to grips with the basics of the human experience. They are likely to be hard and often short lived. Baby souls find themselves buffeted by many of the most negative experiences that life has to offer. Few baby lifetimes should be necessary for most souls.

Young souls react to a need not to experience the tribulations of baby soul lifetimes again. These lifetimes are characterised by great aspiration for success, material acquisitiveness, the pursuit of power in many forms, and the desire for fame or even notoriety. There is a seductive quality about young lifetimes since they seem to offer so much and thus it may be difficult to break free of them.

Midterm lifetimes may form the majority of incarnations a soul experiences. Relatively, these are 'ordinary' lifetimes wherein the quantity of higher self energy allows enough for the individual to experience moderate success in their lives in a way that does not distract them from their soul's development. At the end of this cycle, a realisation comes upon the soul that there is more that needs to be understood and that the way in which they have viewed the lives and their purpose may have been missing something.

Old souls specifically desire that they should move on as quickly as possible from their third dimensional existence and therefore will begin to actively search for truths beyond those presented within the conventions of society. Lifetimes may be spent simply searching and following blind alleys until they come upon the awareness that the ability to ascend is within them and must begin from a very third dimensional perspective of achieving balance.

How many lifetimes are there at each soul level?

We may spend innumerable lifetimes in any one of these phases. It is not until we have mastered the experiences of any one level that we are able to move on to the next.

What is a soul purpose?

Each one of us is a unique soul and we have a purpose that is a part of the essence of our being encoded in our soul DNA. It affects every lifetime that we experience, and to some degree or another it affects the way we live our lives and what we do. Purposes may be explained generically as roles and they include artisans, warriors, musicians, teachers, healers and many more. It is also known as a soul type.

<u>What is soul DNA?</u>

Soul DNA is an encoding that is not within our physical form. It is perpetually with us and does not change as we move from body to body via reincarnation.

In much the same way that the other forms of DNA are a storehouse for genetic information, soul DNA is a storehouse for that which relates to our spiritual selves. It records our previous lifetimes, our soul's purpose and soul contracts that we have entered into.

<u>What are soul contracts?</u>

A soul contract is an agreement made by a being before it incarnates relating to a particular lifetime. Some lifetimes, particularly those of the younger soul levels may have no contracts associated with them; but it is likely that the older a soul gets, the more it agrees to undertakings of various kinds. These commitments are usually in relation to the way in which we will help and support others in their learning and involve activity of every conceivable kind. They always involve achievements that are for the highest good of all.

<u>Why were the guides with me?</u>

These four were indeed, as I had originally hoped, angels. Their purpose for being with me was specifically to assist me in the development of latent abilities that I possessed to channel. This ability had been with me since birth and before. Across numerous lifetimes I had been a channel. In fact it was my soul purpose to channel and bring forth information for others as a teacher of spiritual matters.

Deeply imbedded within what they referred to as my 'soul's DNA' was all of the knowledge that I needed to perform this task. I just didn't realise it yet.

During my late teen years I had suffered from a number of epileptic type fits but after much medical testing, I was cleared of being epileptic and their cause remained a mystery. The fits ceased to affect me after I had only had half a dozen of them. The angels related that these had been a necessary 'rewiring' of my brain at this time in preparation for what was happening now. As I became stronger as a channel further 'rewirings' would be necessary, but these would take a different form.

When I was sufficiently comfortable with what I was going through and when I was strong enough in my abilities, another being would come and take over the teaching. By 'strong' they meant able to tune in effortlessly to what they termed their 'vibration'. By 'comfortable', they meant that I could accept what was happening to me.

The great irony in all of this was that the stronger I became, the more uncomfortable I became. The information they gave me struck me on the one hand as knowledge I had always known that was second nature to me; on the other it was absolutely bizarre. I began to feel that perhaps I was falling prey to some form of schizophrenia or becoming a sociopath. Their reassurances that their communication with me was not a result of me becoming delusional did little to help.

Oddly, Sharon had more confidence in what was going on than I did. In fact she seemed to think it was all rather normal and talked about the four as if they were flesh and blood. She would ask me how I had got on today and what we'd talked about. Repeatedly I would ask her if it ever occurred to her that I was making the whole thing up, but she never did. On other days I would tell her that I thought I was going crazy but she would just smile patiently and tell me not to be silly.

One day the angels asked me if I would like to be in the presence of the one who would continue my teaching and I willingly agreed. Immediately I experienced a vast presence that left me breathless and feeling that I was being forced back into my chair. The sense of power was overwhelming, but so was the sense of benevolence and peace. This, they said, was Archangel Michael. When I was receptive to his coming, he would speak through me.

An avatar is here

The conversations with the angelic guides continued for several months and so did the teaching. At one point they began to explain their experience of being to me:

As beings of light they do not have the same sensory or emotional capacity that humans do. Whilst we might think of angels as exceptionally lucky and gifted, their range of experience is much more limited than ours. The sensations of the third dimension are something of a mystery to them and they aspire to know them in order that they are more effective in performing their support role. Very few actually get the chance to. Those who do are able to because they have the opportunity to walk the earth as avatars.

If you believe that an avatar is something from a TV show, a virtual reality image or even a persona on a computer you could certainly be forgiven for harbouring this belief. Modern interpretations of the word have somehow lost the origins, although in the Hindu belief system the concept of a deity incarnating in the body of an animal is still well known. And this is what they were describing.

Living a full human lifetime is not possible for angels; even occupying a human body or appearing in human form is something that happens very rarely and for the briefest periods of time. If angels wish to live a whole lifetime, they may only do so by occupying the body of an animal 'for the duration' so to speak; but even then there are very limited opportunities. It is difficult and it has great risk of hardship attached to it.

The angel usually enters the body of the animal shortly after it is born, displacing the soul that was waiting to live that lifetime. (If this seems cruel, understand that it is absolutely painless and the incumbent's life energy is then immediately back at the front of the line for incarnating in another body within micro-seconds.) Like human beings, its knowledge of what it is and all memories are usually lost shortly after birth. If they are able to incarnate in this way there is always a specific purpose attached to that lifetime. Such as the one being performed by the avatar that was with us now.

This revelation sent me reeling. There was an avatar living with us? Here? Now? I saw nothing in the least bit angelic about the dogs as they all seemed quite normal to me. Which one?

Dougal.

The guides explained that it was his purpose to provide protection for me. When someone is learning to be an open channel (which is what, they said, I was to become), in their early development they need to establish a connection with higher realms and vibrations. As they become more open, unwelcome energies can enter into their vibration and subvert them from their purpose, giving inaccurate information and damaging their ability to develop their potential as a messenger for the highest good.

What does it mean: 'For the highest good'?

As individuals we tend to view our actions as being isolated in their effects i.e. we are only conscious of their impact upon those who are connected in some way to the circumstances of an event.

Each and every action is compromised of an intention and an outcome. Both the intention and the outcome create a vibration. The vibrations go far beyond the immediacy of the circumstances. They carry outwards into the world at large and effect what can be termed the collective consciousness.

When we act for the highest good, in essence it means that there is no harm in what we do and the vibration created is beneficial to all.

In this context Dougal's presence ensured that the messages that I would be able to deliver could only be beneficial.

Knowing that I would become open to channelling at this time, the angel that had become the avatar Dougal had made a commitment that he would come to be with us to protect me from these energies. The power of his angelic presence acted as a dampening field to negative energies and prevented them from getting through to me.

He would do this up until the point where I was strong enough to cope by myself and would no longer need him. He didn't necessarily perform this task knowingly since it was his very presence that caused the effect; but he was filling his purpose admirably and my progress as a channel was thus far smooth and uninterrupted. When the task was complete, he would be able to enjoy the pleasures of just being a dog, but he would always be able to provide this protection whilst he was near me.

Once again, I was stunned and a little incredulous. How was it possible? The angels reminded me of my sense that he almost recognised me when we first saw him; and the strange sensation that he was supposed to come home with us. But if he was meant to be with us all along, why had he come via such a convoluted route? Surely we had gotten him by chance?

They assured me that there was no such thing where a matter of this importance was concerned. It had always been intended that he would perform this role, but his route to us was difficult on an intentional, albeit necessary basis:

- We would not have chosen a GBGV as a first breed of dog; it could only have been Kaiti because no other breed would have captivated me in the way the Shar Pei had.
- We would not have chosen a GBGV as a companion for Kaiti as we didn't know the breed and Kaiti (seemed to) like gundogs.
- We would not have got a third dog that was any bigger than Emily because Sharon wanted a small dog and despite the fact that the breeder bred both Petits and Grands, the larger dogs were never in contention.
- He couldn't come to us as a puppy because we would never have dreamed of taking another puppy at that time.

- The idea of a fourth dog had not filtered into our consciousness and wouldn't have. Three was considered outrageous by anybody we met, so we kind of went along with that train of thought.
- We had agreed that we would not have a male dog, since although all of our girls were spayed, we believed males to be generally more work.
- He had to arrive via a known and trusted person (Viv).
- He had to arrive at a specific point in our lives where we would be receptive to another dog.
- And he had to have a hard luck story.

It all started to make some sense, but now I wanted to understand more fully about the nature of avatars, so another question and answer session followed:

Are all avatars dogs?

No, but there is a preponderance of avatars in dog form. This comes about because of how easily dogs are accepted by mankind and integrated into their lives. Smaller numbers come as horses. Preferred bodies used to be cats and it should be noted that in Ancient Egypt cats were revered because the Egyptians believed that many cats would be incarnate angels! They even deified them, hence the cat goddess Bast. These days, cats are a little out of favour because their relationship to humans does not allow them the same degree of acceptance afforded to dogs. This being the case it is therefore quite odd that some also come as rats, although there is a very good reason for this.

What is the purpose of an avatar?

Aside from the physical experience that has already been discussed, avatars arrive with a specific purpose that will relate to the lives of those who they are meant to be with. Dougal's tale illustrates that the path to that person is not always straightforward, but they will get to where they are meant to be. The purpose is utterly unique to the person and the avatar and cannot be generalised. In the tales that follow, more very specific purposes will be revealed.

Why can't their role be performed by 'normal' dogs?

In all cases their purpose relates to that which they are able to achieve as angelic beings of light that they could not do otherwise. Dougal's ability to act as a 'dampening field' could not be replicated by the average member of the canine population. An avatar's energies are far and above that of a third dimensional dog.

How many avatars are there?

Avatars are quite rare. Only around .0003% or one in three thousand - of all dogs occupying the planet at any one time are angelic beings. The number is even less in other species.

How can you recognise an avatar?

You can't! There will be absolutely no outward evidence that there is anything special about them whatsoever. However, they will have a very specific energy about them.

How do avatars behave?

Just because an avatar is the embodiment of an angel, that doesn't necessarily mean that it will act like one! The pressures of being an avatar can be great if only because they are trying to squeeze their angelic energy into an earth bound third dimensional body. It is not always an easy or comfortable thing and they respond to the pressures of living accordingly. An avatar is actually *less* likely to appear angelic than other dogs because of this.

There is also the dimension of their purpose that needs to be added to the equation: Depending upon the nature of its purpose the characteristics displayed by an avatar may be anything from otherworldly to totally doglike! In fact sometimes their tasks involve being highly canine.

The very fact they are being given the opportunity to be an avatar means that they are actually *more* likely to be doglike just to get the experience and frankly, have fun.

Do avatars know what they are?

Avatars come into the world with varying degrees of consciousness of what they are. For the most part they have no knowledge whatsoever (although I do now know of two 'fully conscious' avatars). Their consciousness is related to their tasks; if the nature of the task requires them to intercede immediately, they will know exactly what they are and what they have to do.

If this is not the case they are likely to undergo a transformation at some point in their lives when they need to fulfil their purpose. This may bring about a permanent change in their awareness of themselves that is demonstrable within their character; or it may be a temporary alteration that lasts a matter of minutes.

Do avatars recognise one another?

They have even less knowledge of each other than they do of themselves. For them it is the equivalent of the way in which we humans regard them. They look just the same as ordinary dogs and are indistinguishable. They are cognoscent of their energies being different, but they have no explanation for it.

Do avatars know of their purpose?

Like humans, they have their purpose within their soul DNA but it is rare that they are permitted to remember it at birth. It will come to them when required and they will respond accordingly because they get more input from their higher selves than we do. But essentially an avatar is still allowed to be the creature it has come in as, because that is what it wanted/needed to experience.

When I relayed the information to Sharon we marvelled at the convoluted ways of the universe. We were both saddened and moved by the experience that the avatar Dougal was prepared to go through in order to get to us. It slowly began to dawn on us that there was something much bigger going on than we had hereto imagined.

An unexpected Christmas present: Molly & Daisy's tale

Even before we knew what he really was, Dougal was already a massive hit in our household. His generally easygoing nature and love of company provided a nice balance with Kaiti's diffidence, Pippa's neediness and Emily's independence. Like all of the pack members, he certainly had his moments; but on balance I considered him such a great joy to own that I felt we'd been missing out by not having a Grand Basset Griffon Vendeen before, so now I wanted another! Sharon didn't take too much persuading and only six months after Dougal's arrival, we had arranged with Viv to take delivery of Molly, a female GBGV puppy.

It was almost startling to experience the difference between Molly and Dougal since although they were physically similar, temperamentally they were like chalk and cheese. Whereas Dougal was laid back and easy going, Molly was uptight and frantic. On walks she would howl for the hunt, encouraging the others to join in with her wild chases after any scent that she came across.

On one occasion her passion for scenting got her into trouble when, whilst out walking in the woods, she strayed too far from me. I could not find her and returned the other dogs to the safety of the car so that I could focus on her. I searched for the next 15 minutes until, from a raised bank, I could see her in a clearing a great distance away. Coming towards her from the opposite direction were two youths on a miniature motorbike, being ridden illegally in the woods. Molly was too far away to be recalled or protected and she was paralysed with fear. As they careened past her the rasping engine of the crude machine spat fumes and smoke so close to her that she turned and fled in terror. I was livid and ran towards the bikers. As the distance between us closed I picked up a large branch and it was just as well that they headed up another track just before I got to them or I swear I would have knocked them off whilst they were in motion.

Molly was nowhere to be seen and for the next hour I hunted high and low, calling at the top of my voice. The woods covered a vast acreage and there was no sign or sound of my lost dog. I was rapidly approaching the time when I would have to pick up Jenny from the school bus, so with great reluctance and considerable stress, I drove away.

It was half an hour later before I was able to return with Sharon and we recommenced the search. Within minutes we caught sight of Molly running backwards and forwards between the trees, still clearly terrified. She seemed to be totally unable to recognise us and she was whining pitifully. Eventually with gentle coaxing we managed to persuade her to come to us and we were greeted with pathetic gratitude. Although the experience had done nothing to deter her from running manically at the slightest opportunity, from that point onwards she became the only one of the hounds that could be relied upon to always come back.

Over the years, her hunting instincts were honed to the point of perfection; that is: perfection in recognising a scent and making one hell of a racket when she does smell something gamey. Molly, despite immense speed and agility has never actually managed to catch anything. She is very keen on squirrel chasing and will sit for literally hours underneath a tree watching the bushy tailed rodents as they play tantalisingly out of her reach. She will spot harmless creatures from ridiculous distances away and set up her baying call. She can whip the rest of the dogs into a frenzy of excitement and instigate a full pursuit of what is apparently nothing at all in seconds. But thankfully, she is a total failure as a hunter.

For a few weeks we were a five dog, two cat household. However, it was only for a few weeks.

The day before Christmas Eve, Viv emailed to ask if we would consider taking Daisy, a Grand Basset that had been returned to her in somewhat tragic circumstances. Her owner had cancer and wished to spend his last days travelling which, with two dogs, he could not do. Therefore Daisy and her housemate Boo had been returned to Viv as per the purchase agreement. Any unwanted dog, no matter what age, Viv would take back. Fortunately for Boo, he quickly fell on his feet and was taken in by a widow who had recently lost her husband. She doted on him and they formed a very happy partnership that sustains to this day. Daisy was not so fortunate. After a couple of weeks with Viv she was rehomed with a couple who had a young family and a spaniel. The spaniel was an aggressive dog and attacked Daisy who was in turn blamed for causing trouble. At some subsequent point, their young child grabbed Daisy and squeezed her, hard. In response Daisy snapped and that was enough for the family to return her to Viv.

In desperation she emailed us and we drove to her house in the cold dark evening. We met Daisy in the kitchen and up until that point I had never experienced a more wretched and sad looking dog. She was an unusually small GBGV who was clearly very distressed by the experiences of the past few weeks and was doubtless missing Boo who had been her lifelong companion. She had a deep scar on the top of her head where the spaniel had attacked her and she clearly lacked anything that now resembled confidence. Our hearts went out to her and of course, she came home with us.

Daisy was the most fearful of any of the dogs we had taken into our home and during her first few hours with us, she slunk around, unable to settle anywhere. The other dogs sensed her discomfort and she began to annoy them by constantly moving around. She would come in close to them whilst they were attempting to sleep, most likely craving the warmth and comfort of a friendly companion to snuggle up to. We were immensely shocked when Pippa, normally the most placid of all of our dogs, snapped at her as she walked by. Assuming a dominant position, she growled fiercely and showed a frightening array of teeth to the much smaller dog. Daisy was clearly terrified and hid herself between the back of my legs and the armchair I was sitting in. She peeped up at me with pleading eyes and her expression seemed to hold a mixture of misery and desperation. For the briefest of moments I was sure that I heard a voice in my head imploring me to help her.

That night Daisy became the third dog to sleep in our room. Kaiti was next to me, Dougal next to Sharon and Daisy at the foot of the bed. The next morning when the dogs were let out she went to the garden gate and sat in front of it. She put her head back and let out a single howl. It was the most mournful and heartbreaking sound that I have ever heard. It went on for many moments and when she had poured out all of her grief in this way, she sat with her head hanging down for the longest time. We guessed that at that moment she wanted Boo and she wanted

69

her humans. She wanted the familiarity of her home and everything she had known. It brought tears to our eyes.

It was to take over a year before Daisy finally settled with us. Whilst she never made that tragic sound again, we would catch her looking depressed and soulful on many occasions over the coming months. Certain attributes of her previous home life became obvious as time went by: she had been used to sleeping with her people on their bed; she was a lap dog and liked to be cuddled; she had been used to sharing packets of chips with her owners; she always lay underneath their dining table as they ate. Undoubtedly her life with us was a stark contrast. We indulged her as much as we could without alienating the others and for several years she remained the only dog that was allowed to come onto the sofa for a cuddle. In other areas we would not compromise, if only for her own good.

A few weeks after we had taken Daisy into our home, we were contacted by her previous owner who expressed a desire to see Daisy one more time. Although we felt that this would be very unfair on both of them, we tentatively agreed and then spent a great deal of time worrying about the implications of this decision. It had been left that he would contact us after his return from travelling but we never heard from him again. I have to say that I was very grateful for this because I believe that witnessing the emotional turmoil that it would have inevitably caused for both man and beast would have been heart wrenching beyond belief.

Although today Daisy is a totally different animal, the animosity between her and Pippa has never gone away. Whilst Pippa has never repeated her initial reaction, Daisy still makes sure that she keeps a respectful distance at all times. She retains a great deal the behavioural characteristics that come from her former life, particularly her passion for chips and a need to be cuddled. She is certainly not the most confident of our dogs, but she is now a quirky but very happy and loving little creature.

In contrast with Pippa's response, Kaiti seemed to accept Daisy straight away and at that point, it was interesting for us to note that although Kaiti is not exactly what you'd call 'a dog's dog' (such is her level of indifference to all those around her) she was never fazed by the introduction of the dogs who had followed her into our household. Quite the opposite, she was always the first to accept them.

You have how many dogs?

You might think that from a child's perspective, having so many pets around might be like living in some kind of animal paradise; but between Kaiti's arrival and Daisy's arrival on the scene, over seven years had passed. The children were now fourteen and ten and frankly, they wondered what all of the fuss was about pets. Whilst their friends might have viewed their situation with envy, this glut of animals seemed perfectly normal to our children. The dogs certainly provided moments of immense fun, frivolity and companionship, but they could also be a lot of hard work. It is ironic to us that so many kids crave canine company whilst ours had to be practically blackmailed in order to get them to accompany us on walks!

Walking the pack became an exercise in logistics all by itself. If we took them to the wood, which was their favourite outing, each had to be loaded into our SUV which sat on the driveway outside our yard fence. If they went out of the back gate unleashed, the hounds would bound away and disappear from sight in an instant. But once in the back of the car, if the back was opened to admit other dogs, those already inside would also try to get away. Many was the time that Sharon and I would play an interesting game of 'herd the doggies'; and even upon our return, despite an exhausting jaunt, the BGVs would try to dash away when the mood took them. Local walks were somewhat easier. I could just about manage all six by myself using multiple connecting leashes; but it was always easier if Sharon accompanied me. The BGVs were quite a sight, all harnessed like a Siberian Husky race team (although the irony of this observation would not strike me for many years to come) and they would certainly pull like one. Walking through the area where we lived, I imagine that we were often mistaken for professional dog walkers.

Encouraged by Viv, and since four of the pack were members of the breed, we joined the Basset Griffon Vendeen Club. As a family outing we attended their summer fun day with the appropriate dogs. The other members found us something of a novelty that we had four BGVs (so it was anybody's guess what they might have thought if we'd told them about the other two!) but they were a very friendly bunch. The fun day always culminated in a 'show' with many humorous judging classes and we would each take a dog as our entry for the day. With so many dogs we were bound to win at least one prize, but we found ourselves taking many second and third places in such categories as 'dog with the longest eyelashes (Emily was robbed, hers were the longest!); dog with the best hard luck story; dog that looks most like their owner. However, we were very proud that in the last year that we attended, Daisy (being shown by Tristan) won the overall grand prize for best dog in show.

Occasionally the pack's harmonious existence could be unsettled which consequently cause trouble for us, as events proved one New Year's Eve. A family of German's had moved into a house opposite us during the course of the year and without any warning whatsoever, they chose to celebrate New Year in the way that Germans do: they let off fireworks. And lots of them! The affect on the dogs was instant and devastating. Every single one of them was terrified and they chose to demonstrate their fear by trying to get as close to us as possible. Since we had already gone to bed, this involved jumping on the bed, scratching wildly at doors trying to get to us (as Pippa, Emily and Molly slept downstairs in the kitchen) and, if we stood up, trying to climb up us. By morning we needed a repaint in the kitchen and my legs were a mass of deep and painful scratches.

You could be forgiven for believing that having so many dogs in such a small space as our twelve hundred square foot home would make our lives intolerable, but oddly enough we barely seemed to notice. There was an incredibly cosy feeling to settling down in front of the television at night with all of the dogs spread around. The only negative effects of being a six dog household related to the reactions of others. For some people, the experience was just too much. One day we were visited by a business colleague of mine who, upon being greeted at the door by an overly enthusiastic welcoming committee, actually declined to come into the house.

The dogs did prove to be an in-law deterrent. We lived just under an hour's drive away from my wife's family and they were regular visitors to our house, usually coming up to see us every other weekend. As I have already said, my father in law adored Kaiti and she would even get invited to their house when we visited them. Both of Sharon's parents found Pippa tolerable because she was so wiling and co-operative; but they had started to have reservations about our extended family when Emily arrived. Her naughtiness and disobedience found little favour in their eyes and what we regarded as cute, they found simply undesirable. Dougal was even more difficult for them to cope with, not because of his nature, but his size and enthusiasm; then after Molly and Daisy, it was all just too much. Their visits rapidly decreased in number until if we saw them six times a year, it was unusual. Every cloud...

There was also the added problem of what was going on in the rest of our world. We knew that the channelling would have met with scorn and derision at best, possibly even horror; so we concealed it from Sharon's parents totally. In the meantime, Sharon had pursued an interest in healing that she had since her university days and had been undergoing a series of workshops to become an energy healer using a technique called Quantum Touch. She found that she possessed a great talent for this and went on to become an instructor as well as being a practitioner. A small but loyal client base developed and Sharon found that she was able to bring a great deal of relief to those who were suffering.

What is energy healing?

There exist all around us many forms of energy that flow both within and without our bodies. If these energies are directed (or channelled) through an individual's body and into another, with the correct intention they may bring about healing in another.

However, it is actually the person who received the energies that does the healing. To do this they must be prepared to receive the flow and have an intention within themselves that corresponds to that of the healer i.e. they must want to get better!

Although this may sound silly, not everyone who is ill wants to be well. For some, sickness is a refuge and an excuse for being a victim and letting others exercise control over their lives. To allow this makes things easier for them. It alleviates the burden of personal responsibility and accountability for the self.

My guides had already explained that anybody can heal themselves and others. Natural healing energies have always been around and within us; but focusing them so as to maximise their effectiveness takes patience, concentration and commitment. Whilst anyone might have the potential to do it, far fewer bring the caring required for truly effective application. This, Sharon had in abundance.

It was a source of sadness for Sharon that her gifts were greeted with disinterest and denial by her parents. In some ways it created an unnecessary rift between them as she felt rejected or even scorned by their response. In many ways as it turned out, this helped in what was to come. But for the moment it just seemed unfortunate that as we grew in pleasure at our lives with the animals and the services that we were able to perform, her relationship with her parents took a corresponding downturn.

We were grateful that almost the reverse of these circumstances applied with my parents. I explained the channelling to them with considerable embarrassment but was pleased to discover that they were quite intrigued and open to it. As for the healing, they embraced it with open arms and both became clients of Sharon's. She was even able to effect changes in them from great distances and would regularly perform distance healing upon them, despite the fact that they lived two hours away from us. My father became a great advocate for her and remains so, although he regards the channelling as far less tangible, despite seeking angelic guidance on occasion!

As for their relationship with the dogs, they had by now begun to relax a little more with them and although they found the dog's mad dash to greet them as off-putting as the next person, once the initial frenzy was over, even my committed cat-loving mother began to appreciate the positive aspects of our doggie world.

Sharon's rapidly developing healing skill had benefits for the dogs as well as for clients. If they sustained injuries whilst out walking, Sharon was able to minister to their needs without the need for an expensive vet's bill.

Our life had already developed a routine that revolved around the dog's need for exercise and the woods near our home provided a wonderful place of exploration for them. At first we would let them all run freely, but the hounds would go further and further from us on each walk. Although they always seemed to be able to track us and would return when fatigue took over, we would regularly lose sight of them for half an hour at a time. One day Dougal did not return. He was normally pretty good and his absence was very disturbing.

Finally we heard a deep and mournful baying in the distance and after an extensive search, saw Dougal coming towards us dragging his front left leg. Clearly he had made a jump and hurt himself on impact, or maybe he had even been kicked by one of the deer in the woods. We ran to him and Sharon instantly went to work running energy into his body.

When she perceived that he could take no more I picked him up and carried him back to the car. It was 1km away and Dougal is a very heavy dog. The effort nearly killed me and finally, with the car in sight, I had to put him down to take a rest.

I was less than impressed when he bounded off towards the parked vehicle with total ease. He showed no signs of stiffness or pain and the dragging limb was a thing of the past. From that point onwards I had even more faith in what Sharon could do for the animals!

Angels *and* Masters

About four months after we got Daisy, my four channelling angels suddenly left and never returned. I am still saddened that at the very moment that this happened, I forgot their names and have never been able to recall them; a most odd thing for me. However, in their wake came Archangel Michael. The process of coming to know him was fascinating. My initial feelings of awe at his presence and being humbled that a being as great as an Archangel would allow himself to be channelled through me didn't find much favour with him! He was very quick to point out that we are one and the same thing, from the same source and of the same substance; only our experiences distinguished between us. He regarded me as an equal and insisted that I reciprocate. His manner was open and familiar, and although in nearly all things related to emotion he appeared totally neutral, Michael certainly tried to demonstrate empathy. In comparison with the four guides, he had a much more clearly defined personality; and curiously, he obviously had a sense of humour.

After a very short time he requested that I push back the boundaries of the service I was performing and from that point onward, the whole nature of my channelling underwent a radical transformation. He requested that instead of speaking in my head, I now allow him to speak *through* me. This would involve utilising my voice box whilst I absented myself from my body. Sharon was to act as my audience and he would relay information to her that she could then record.

This was a very daunting prospect indeed and it took me weeks of trying before I was able to let go enough control for this to happen. The experience almost defies description and I can only say that at first it felt a bit like somebody was jumping into my body. It was very uncomfortable and frightening and took a long time to get used to. Once Michael was there, I would hear words that I instantly forgot and see pictures that, I quickly learnt, related to what was being said. I could see people and places; images that seemed to represent concepts; other planets and worlds; historical events; lifetimes passing by in an instant. There seemed to be no end to what I was being exposed to.

At first these sessions were brief. After five minutes I would be tired and totally 'spaced out' and have difficulty feeling myself connected to my body. 'Ungrounded' is the term I came to know. Gradually I became more accustomed to the experience, but then Michael would extend the amount of time that he was speaking through me and further adjustments to my state of being would be necessary.

After several weeks Michael revealed that he would like me to try channelling other beings. By now I was a little more confident so it didn't take too much to persuade me. However, when we were visited by other Archangels, I was surprised at how different the sensation was. Their energy and even their method of entering my body varied from being to being. Sharon was also quite surprised at how different they were. When Michael spoke his voice was very similar to mine but Archangel Raphael had a slightly deeper voice; Gabriel's was softer, another's louder or more forceful. They explained that it was an issue of how they were able to utilise my vocal chords and with practice, each became more proficient at communicating through me. Over time, Sharon could recognise their individual voices without them making their customary introduction of themselves.

The big shock came when I started to channel what were described as Ascended Masters. These were beings that had been human and had, across the course of many lifetimes, managed to fulfil their criteria for learning and soul progression. Now they chose to help those on their ascension pathway rather than move on to their next learning roles. They assumed the presence of one of their incarnations and spoke with accents. Sharon became well accustomed to speaking with individuals from the Far East, Middle East, India, Tibet and others. They weren't just men either! When a lady master visited, very significant changes in my voice occurred. Again, the ability to manipulate my vocal chords was a matter of practice and some managed this easily whilst others struggled at first. In particular, an Egyptian Master named Serapis Bey who visited very frequently was unable to get a consistent accent out of my voice box!

The physical experience of channelling masters was quite unlike that of channelling the angels. The energies were more difficult to manage in their after effect and I would frequently be very tired after their visits.

However, this did not prevent their experimentation with pushing back the boundaries of how long I could hold their energies; nor did it affect my willingness to try. In their presence I rarely stirred physically, and upon their exit, I would often find my body wracked with pain and cramps, as well as being dehydrated.

At one point Michael asked me to try 'fully conscious channelling': the simultaneous existence of both his presence and mine in my body. Whilst it was fascinating (since it allowed me to see the audience i.e. Sharon through their eyes), they were unable to get my blink reflex to work and the entire session was done without any eye movement at all. By the end my eyes had completely dried up and were extremely painful. It also looked, according to Sharon, very creepy as I appeared to be blankly staring in a most unnatural way. I've never done it again since.

Through these sessions, a vast amount of information was revealed to us and we began to get into the practice of both asking for and receiving guidance about all sorts of issues. They would be very careful not to reveal any information about the future and any guidance offered was utterly neutral if it came from the angels themselves. They would certainly make it known if things were 'meant to be', but beyond that, if we needed more specific information around which there were issues of free will, we would have to ask a Master. They would invariably be more forthright. However, with both angels and Masters, our freedom of choice in all matters was always emphasised.

The training process seemed to go well. Getting to grips with who was who was sometimes difficult because many of the angels had strange and unfamiliar names that had not been featured in the books that I had read. Interestingly, they explained that the need for naming them was a very human thing since they considered themselves to all be one and the same. Having walked the earth, many of the Masters could be looked up on the internet and extensively researched.

By the time Michael announced that my training was complete, I had channelled at least two dozen different beings, some repeatedly; and although they would always be the ones to determine who was going to visit with me on any particular occasion, I was now told that we could ask to speak to any one of them at will. I was also asked if I would be prepared to be an 'open' channel. This meant that they could tap into my consciousness to give me information at any time, without having to wait for me to initiate the contact. At first I feared this meant that I would perpetually be hearing voices in my head; but they reassured me that I would have the capability to 'turn it off' at will. However, they could 'turn it back on' if it was important to do so.

Over time we came to trust pretty much everything that we heard. Certainly there were situations when the information coming to us seemed non-sensical or too farfetched for words. Mostly however, this was an issue of ego. For instance, when Michael told us that everything that I had done in my career to date had merely been a preparation for what I was to do with the information I was being given now, I was horrified. When he then went on to say that in my work I already channelled information, with the implication being that it was pretty much all I did, I was indignant!

It was certainly true to say that across the course of my career, I had developed a somewhat unique ability to deliver material. It was a point of great pride with me that I never needed to use notes. Nor did I prepare for a session unless it involved development exercises; and even these I could conjure up, seemingly at will, out of nowhere. I would turn up to run a week long training course with nothing more than a flimsy outline plan, usually written on a scrappy piece of paper. I would have no idea of what I would say and then just stand there and extemporise. Yet I would get outstanding results and had achieved success far in excess of even my own expectations.

"Where", Michael asked, "did I think this ability came from?" I squirmed for a little while before conceding that words just seemed to come into my head. In fact I was never at a loss for words, never floored by a question, and never short of the ability to fill the remit a client had given me. "*All* channelled" he said. Reluctantly I had to admit that in hindsight, it was obvious. But it still took a lot for me to swallow my pride and admit that I was more charmed than brilliant.

It occurred to me when I was given this information that I was only now agreeing to become an open channel and it had to be with my express consent. Yet Michael had previously told me that when I presented in the workplace I was channelling. How was it possible when at that time I did not even know what channelling was and certainly had not given permission? It was explained – as if it were obvious - that of course, I had been channelling my higher self.

What is a higher self?

We all have a higher self. It is the direct source from which we come and is in turn a sub division of an angelic being. It is us in our purest light form, but there are many aspects to it or, if you prefer, beings that come from it. These are all parts of us and may be incarnated at the same time as us although they are equally as likely to be in another time in another galaxy, far, far away! These are known as our 'twin flames'. This is not the same as the romantic notion of a soul mate. In fact, if you were to meet them, you are as likely to be repelled by them as you are to be attracted to them.

You return to your higher self when you are transitioning between one life and the next. At this point you become part of it and are therefore privy to all of the experiences and knowledge gained across all of your lifetimes as well as that of all of your twin flames across all of their lifetimes. As you may imagine, the volume of information and wisdom is vast.

Whilst we are incarnated, our higher self basically has a watching brief over us. It plays no direct part in our lives but is something that we can get in contact with so as to receive advice, wisdom and guidance. A lot of what people dismiss as instinct or gut feeling is really their higher self talking to them. It is because of our high level of sentience and absolute right to our freedom of choice that our higher self has no direct ability to influence our lives. However, if you are open to it, you have the capability to receive the wisdom it may impart to you via your subconscious, which is the part of your brain that maintains contact.

When I am presenting, quite unconsciously, I receive information from my higher self to my great benefit. Somewhat unusually I had already developed this ability by the time I began channelling. This is why I was

---

able to hear the voice in my head saying "May I?" with such ease and clarity. Although it was not my higher self speaking to me at that point, the access point was open that allowed this contact. It didn't make me special. It was simply what I had always done in previous lifetimes and had committed to do in this one!

Often there was information that was so surprising that we would ask for a ratification of what we were hearing to be given to us in our physical realm three times before we would accept it. Every time we asked for this, without exception, it was given. So when on Christmas Eve in 2003 it suddenly came into Sharon's head that we were 'meant' to emigrate and Michael confirmed it in a channelling session, you might understand why we still asked for three pieces of ratification. Within hours we had all three.

Another country

Since I began my global travelling in 1996 I had felt increasingly unsettled every time I returned to the UK. There was just something in me that felt like I was in the wrong place, but persuading Sharon that we should emigrate was a task of almost insurmountable difficulty. She had a large family presence in the country, whereas mine consisted of just my parents, most of my relatives having died in the previous five years. What began as a subtle process of influence almost turned into a war of attrition as I became more and more unhappy with living in the country.

Finally, in 2002 I had persuaded Sharon that we should at least consider moving someplace else. I was about to leave on what would become my last world tour and we agreed that upon my return, we would draw up a shortlist of potential destinations. When we did it included Australia, New Zealand, Singapore and Dubai; all places where English was commonly spoken. I had visited all of these places on the trip and on this occasion had intentionally viewed them from a homemaking perspective. I had also stopped on the west coast of Canada but ruled it out as despite the fact that I was quite enamoured of the place, I was convinced that Sharon would find Vancouver dull.

We didn't get far beyond the shortlist because Sharon constantly stalled. My agitation didn't let up however and I managed to convince her that during our channelling session with the lady in America, we should ask where would be the best place for us to go and so we did. The answer we received was somewhat neutral but she ruled out Singapore and said that Australia had potential.

As an indirect consequence we undertook the complex and not inexpensive qualifications vetting procedure necessary before making a full application for landed immigrant status in Australia. All had gone well and after many months of waiting and countless hours of work on my part, our forms were ready for submission. The night the documents lay in their sealed envelope waiting for me to take them to the post office, the coming attractions adverts on television showed that there was a programme that very evening with the catchy title: 'Ten things that can kill you in Australia'. I didn't see it but Sharon did and after that submitting the application would only ever have been an exercise in futility. There was no way she was living there!

For a long while I teetered on the edge of desperation induced depression, so strong was my feeling that we needed to leave. So when on that fateful Christmas Eve morning as we were driving to her parents house for the routine celebration, Sharon made the wild suggestion that we move to Canada, I was like a pig in clover. There had been no mention of or discussion about emigration for months. The comment came totally out of the blue: "Let's move to Canada." It had never even been mentioned let alone considered beforehand. At first I thought that she was joking and told her how cruel it would be if she was just saying it as a 'wind up'. She was adamant that she meant it so I floated around for the rest of the day and got past the repetitive boredom that Christmas's had become with consummate ease.

I then proceeded to do absolutely nothing. I did no research. I obtained no application forms. I progressed an application not one iota. Despite Michael's confirmation that it would be for our highest good to go to Canada, and despite the ratifications, I ignored it all. In truth, I had passed believing that my very personal dream of getting out of the UK was really shared by anyone else. Whilst I had relished the moment of Sharon's professed desire to emigrate, I felt that to be faced with another last minute refusal would be too much for me. And above all else, I actually felt I needed Sharon to be the driving force behind the move: I did not want to be culpable if she ever came to regret such a monumental change in our lives.

So when in May of the following year Sharon asked me if I had sent in the application forms for Canada yet, my heart skipped several beats. Within a week we had found an immigration agent in Canada and our application had actually been submitted. Our agency was called Avatar and this alone we considered another major sign.

The processing of an immigration application takes years, so we waited for another year and half before we felt that it would be a good idea to begin 'on the ground' research about where we should live. We had of course asked Michael about this, but being unwilling to influence our freedom of choice he would only recommend that we be within a day's drive of Lake Louise, his etheric retreat. He would not be drawn further. This was pretty convenient as we had already decided that we would prefer the west of Canada, but stretching the imagination a little, a day's drive from Lake Louse meant that we could be up to ten hours drive away.

What is an etheric retreat?

An etheric retreat is an area on the planet that resonates with the vibration of the being that is associated with it. Often, but not always, they are in areas of unspoilt natural beauty to which people are drawn for reasons they may not always understand.

In late September I flew to Vancouver and began the search. The irony of beginning in the very place that I had ruled out more than three years beforehand was not lost on me. According to Google maps, you could make it from Vancouver to Lake Louise in nine hours, so anywhere along that route, or even the city itself would be fine. However, this time I felt very uncomfortable even in the periphery of the urban environment and began to drive east. I got as far as central British Columbia, an area known as the Okanagan, before stopping. Sharon had expressed some interest in the area due to the relatively mild climate and I had intended to spend several days there. But once again, the place just didn't feel right; after two days of exploration I continued east.

The provincial border between British Columbia and Alberta is marked with a road sign that says something highly original like 'Welcome to Alberta'. I had never visited Alberta so the experience was a novel one but scenery wise there is no instant change. Basically you transition from trees and mountains to more trees and mountains and but for the road sign, you would not realise that you had changed provinces.

Although it sounds bizarre, the very moment I crossed that notional line, I was overwhelmed with a massive sense of relief and a feeling of having arrived home. I had previously held no beliefs or opinions about Alberta yet the feeling occurred at the very moment I crossed.

Clearly this was where we were meant to be.

Kaiti on our very first day of dog ownership.

At two years, Kaiti already seemed to possess a strange serenity and other worldliness.

Pippa's eyes always seem to show fear that being in a photo might just steal her soul.

A very laid back Emily who looks like she needs a haircut.

Dougal managing to look both adoring and adorable.

Molly in her most typical pose: under a tree about six feet below a mocking red squirrel.

A very sad Daisy, just after we got her.

Jenny and I on our porch in Canada with the newly arrived Indiana Jones.

Emily caught in the act of escape whilst Molly looks on. Fortunately, on this occasion, Tristan was on the other side of the fence waiting to catch her.

Briony already working her magic upon Tristan.

Pippa trying to pretend that the camera isn't really there.

Molly, Emily and Pippa share a rather crowded basket.

Daisy three years on: very happy and enjoying the snow.

Emily, Pippa, Dougal and Kaiti are happy and satisfied after an hour long run around the woods.

A maturing Briony groomed to look like a 'real' (and very attractive) poodle.

Although side by side with Pippa, the distain on Kaiti's face is still obvious and her body language says it all.

Sharon with Dougal and Emily.

Emily, Dougal, Daisy and Molly enjoying the sun in the flatbed of the truck, a much
favoured place.

Indy at 6 months seems nearly as big as Tristan at 12 years.

Dougal gets ready to go for a drive.

Indiana Jones: Indy's tale

When in the month of February prior to my Canadian trip, it was suggested to us that it would be to our great advantage to get another dog before we emigrated, it didn't create too many issues for us. This was mainly because this time we were told that it would be an avatar of great power whose purpose would be revealed to us in time. But to accompany the great power, it would be a dog of great size: a Leonberger no less!

If you are not familiar with the breed, Leonbergers are gentle giants. They have the curious history of being bred because the mayor of a town in Germany wanted a dog that looked like a lion, so a dog was bred complete with mane! They are a rather stunning result of crossing Grand Pyreneans, St Bernards and Newfoundlands; and although they can look every bit as intimidating as any enormous dog, they are essentially pussy cats!

You may recall the earlier tale of Sharon disliking the Leonberger in the dog book? Since that time I had removed the breed from my consciousness so when it was raised again by Michael himself, it was a pleasant surprise. In early 2005 we went specifically to see the Leonbergers at Crufts and fortunately Sharon was smitten when she saw the real thing. We asked for guidance on where this mighty beast was to come from and were directed to a lovely breeder who was planning a litter at the end of the year. We went to meet her at the show and managed to track down a lady who turned out to be as charming and gentle as the massive dogs she was grooming. Deborah was extremely well spoken, perhaps as the English would say, from a 'posh' background and certainly well schooled; but there were no airs and graces about her. She clearly relished the noisy bustle of Crufts and the interactions with the other breeders, many of whom could best be described as 'salt of the earth' types. As we observed the banter that went on and the friendly rivalry, we were struck by the adoration they all obviously felt for their dogs and how levelling their ownership of them was. There was no class system here. The only thing that mattered was that you cared for your dog. She actually apologised for not being able to spend more time talking to us and invited the whole family to come and visit her kennels the following weekend.

The following Sunday we set out on the two hour drive from our home with no real expectation of what type of place we were going to and we were a little shocked to eventually arrive at what looked like a Stately Home complete with security gates and intercom entry system. As we drove up through the splendour of the grounds we could see no sign of Leonbergers, just pristine lawns, orchards and beautiful meadows where horses cantered. We pulled up to a house fronted by an impressive turning circle, already occupied by a motley assortment of vehicles and we realised that we were not the only visitors.

Deborah came out to greet us and as she opened the front door we could hear the voices of several dogs heralding our arrival. She ushered us into the house, apologising for the mess despite the fact that we were in a spotless if slightly Spartanly furnished house.

We were led into a large and comfortable sitting room overlooking a fabulous garden and introduced to her other guests who turned out to be old friends of Deborah's, connected through the Leonberger world. I was very aware of how humble our home was compared with this, and in another context it would have looked like the lady of the manor hosting a tea party for her servants. But with Deborah, it was just a relaxed gathering of equals and she couldn't have done more to make us feel at home. She gave us tea and home baked delights, including the most exquisite chocolate brownies. These were served from fine china cups, saucers and plates which somewhat oddly didn't always match. As I looked around the room, which was also not exactly busy, I began to notice that many items seemed to have been broken at some point and repaired. Furnishings, light fittings and ornaments were all a bit the worse for wear. And then it became clear why as, in pairs, she began to introduce us to her dogs. Bursting into the room, side tables wobbled, vases shook and we found ourselves at eye level with seriously big and powerful creatures. With every tread of their giant paws and movement of their colossal bodies they threatened to break some new item; while their tails cut huge swathes through the air that was suddenly filled with their hot panting breath. Seeing the dogs at close quarters in the confinement of a home was at once awing and a little scary. We became very aware of their size and we began to wonder how we could possibly fit one into a modest dwelling that was already home to six other dogs.

After tea had been enjoyed and the introductions to humans and dogs alike were over Deborah gave us a tour of the grounds. Quite apart from their own room indoors that was roughly half the size of the ground floor of our home, the dogs seemed to have free run of the whole house. Outside she showed us the pristine, lavish but largely unused kennels that she had built specially to comply with UK import laws when she brought her first Leonberger into the country. There was even a swimming pool which was basically for the benefit of the dogs. This was luxury living for pooches, big time!

She let us spend some time with the pair that she intended to mate for her next litter and we got a wonderful opportunity to see firsthand what the temperaments were that would influence the genetics of the puppies. Clearly her whole life was devoted to taking care of these beloved pets and when we came to leave several hours later, it was obvious why we had been guided to such a caring individual.

Over the course of the rest of that year we kept in touch with Deborah at intervals and even visited again to get a 'fix' of Leonberger exposure. Then finally we received the great news that the mother-to-be had conceived and that the puppies would be coming just before Christmas. Our level of excitement rose considerably and we almost counted down the days until we expected news of their birth. But that date came and went and we heard nothing. I sent emails so as not to disturb Deborah at what I imagined must be a very busy time, but received no reply. Finally in desperation, I began ringing but only got an answering machine. Then after over a week of trying to reach her, Deborah finally answered the phone.

The voice that spoke to me was shocking. It was frail and tearful and clearly belonged to a broken woman. The puppies had indeed been born safely and were all doing well, but their birth had been accompanied by great personal difficulty and hardship on both physical and emotional levels that had undoubtedly affected her greatly. The tale that unfolded was one of personal pain and suffering that need not be relayed here.

Suffice it to say that her final words to me were: "I'm sorry but I don't have a puppy for you". She had decided to keep them all.

We were deeply concerned for this lovely and gracious lady and I managed to track down one of her friends. A telephone call reassured us that her state of being wasn't something that she was managing to keep hidden from those closer to her. Both her friends and family were indeed taking good care of her.

There then followed a period of massive confusion for us. Why had we been guided to this point where the ultimate outcome was not as we had been led to believe? Why had such a dreadful set of circumstances befallen Deborah, such an obviously good person? And if we were supposed to get this avatar before we moved to Canada, what were we to do now?

Michael reminded us that even those events that are 'meant to be' can be altered by the action of free will and thus it was in this situation.

Several months passed with no guidance concerning what we should do, so we simply waited. And then during a channelling session Michael announced that we now needed to go to 'the source' to get the avatar.

If that sounds otherworldly, what it actually meant was that we should go to the breeders from whom Deborah had got her dogs in the first place. I was unwilling to pester Deborah to find out who these people were so by tracing the breed lines from which her dogs came on the internet, I was able to discover that 'the source' was the Vom Erlau kennels located in a tiny village in the east of Germany near to the Czech border. We quickly got in touch and I was invited to visit them at my convenience.

It just so happened that at that time I was coaching a number of European business leaders in various countries. I would fly out to spend a day or two with them and their teams every month. Although it was a pain going to Paris one day then Milan or Frankfurt the next, it proved to be immensely convenient that one of my clients was in Vienna. By flying to Salzburg a day before I was due there and renting a car, I would be able to drive to Limbach, visit with the breeder and then go on to Vienna. It was all very convenient!

A couple of weeks later I found myself driving across Bavaria and after a few hours and a few wrong turns (I didn't have a road atlas, just a Google map woefully lacking in detail!) I arrived. The Vom Erlau kennels were located in a traditional looking farmhouse. From the outside, the only evidence that I was at the right place was a very impressive wooden sign. I rang the bell at the outer fence and a diminutive lady opened an inner gate in a high wall. In good but accented English she called to me to come through. As I entered we had a brief moment to introduce ourselves before a tidal wave of Leonbergers came sweeping towards us. I was stunned. I think Deborah had about 8 dogs when we first met her. Giselle had more like 28. They surged around me, buffeting me like a leaf caught in a powerful wind. Some jumped up, placing their enormous paws on my shoulders; some pushed their heads into my butt; others tried to sniff every inch of my body. It was a breathtaking experience.

Finally they all turned and rushed away with the haste of a wave leaving the shore. Giselle's husband, Hubert, had thrown a large quantity of kibble on the ground nearby and clearly the food was a lot more appealing than me. Only one dog remained. He sat with perfect posture looking up at me expectantly. "This" explained Giselle "is Abelard. Abelard will be the father of your puppy and he is our main stud dog. He is waiting because he thinks you have brought another lady for him to cover. This is what many of the visitors to our home come for. When he sees that you do not have such a lady for him he will go. But if you like, you can pretend that you have a camera and see what he does" I mimicked taking out a camera and pretended to photograph Abelard. Instantly he shifted his posture and assumed an incredibly photogenic and handsome pose. Giselle and I laughed. "He does this because he is many times a champion and he is so used to being positioned for photos that he does it all by himself now" she explained. Then sure enough, disappointed in my lack of a female for him, Abelard wandered away.

I found Giselle and Hubert to be even more warm, charming, down to earth and ordinary than Deborah, and they had a tremendous sense of humour. After we had chatted for a while they asked if I would like to go

93

for a walk with the dogs. I willingly agreed but wondered how we would be able to manage so many dogs on leashes. But instead of taking ten minutes preparing to take the dogs out as we usually did at home, Hubert simply opened a wide gate in the fence at the rear of the property and the teeming mass of canines rushed out into the field behind their house totally unfettered. We followed behind and much to my surprise the dogs encircled us. As we wandered out through the fields, no dog ever strayed more than a few metres away. They gambolled like enormous lambs, pretended to fight with each other and occasionally raced back to their humans for attention, barking joyously in mad cacophony. Not for one moment was any of us without a dog to fuss over, in fact we were mostly spoilt for choice.

We reached the summit of a small hill and surveyed the land around us. Three humans and twenty eight mega-dogs paused in the midst of ploughed fields, meadows and woods that stretched as far as the eye could see. "What do the neighbours think of all of the noise?" I asked, looking back towards the village. "Well, there are not too many problems because they are quite quiet for most of the time. But as you can see, on the one side of our house there is the churchyard and the dogs do not wake the dead people." Giselle said with a wicked grin. "And on the other side the house belongs to us and the people who live there rent it from us, so of course they also say nothing." "Does the farmer mind all of these dogs walking across his land?" I asked. "Oh no, all of this land that you can see up to the forests is also ours" she replied in a very matter of a fact way. I hid my surprise well.

A couple of hours and a cup of tea later, Giselle showed me out. As we came to the front gate I noticed for the first time the beautiful land across the road from the farm house and remarked upon it. "Yes it is very nice. It also belongs to us and so do these houses" she said pointing to a row to the right. "So as you can see, it is not a problem to have so many dogs. No?"

We had agreed that Giselle would choose a puppy from the litter on our behalf. By now I totally trusted her judgement and anyway, Michael added that she would be guided to select the right one for us. All we had to do was wait for the litter to be born. But as it turned out, by the time they were born and we could collect our new puppy, his journey home with us would be to Canada, not the UK.

Moving to Canada

In February of 2006 we had taken a family vacation to the spectacular Fairmont Chateau at Lake Louise. It afforded Sharon and the children their first opportunity to see the country we had decided to call home and they were not to be disappointed. In spite of minus 28c degrees temperatures, they were all captivated by the sheer beauty of the countryside and the friendliness of the people. We stayed in adjoining luxurious suites with spectacular views over the lake and we indulged in a whole series of activities that we had never experienced before. We went on a horse drawn sleigh ride, ice skated and snow shoed amidst countryside with fresh air and astounding views. On the fourth day, Sharon and I drove to Bragg Creek where we had arranged to look for houses while the kids did their own thing. On another day, Jenny went to ski school whilst the rest of us hiked. Then as the climax of the holiday, we arranged to go dog sledding. It was a wonderful experience being towed at ground level at great speed by a team of eight dogs. It was only a minor disappointment that they weren't Huskies as we had romantically expected, but nonetheless, great fun. It was to be three years before the irony of this disappointment would strike home. Also, unbeknownst to us in that moment, we had just taken our last family holiday.

On our last day, we drove back to Bragg Creek and viewed even more houses, this time with the kids. By the end of the day we had learnt enough to make some decisions about what we wanted and upon our return to the UK we entered into negotiations on a house. It was a three storey walkout of around 2800 square feet, more than twice the size of our UK property. It came with nearly nine acres of land and was completely enclosed by forest. It was situated off a very quiet highway but you could drive past and never know that it was there. In almost all respects it would make a perfect habitat for a family with dogs. By April the deal was done and completion was due on June 29th. We could move in that day.

As the time for the move came closer we made plans in anticipation of the way things would need to be. The forest that surrounded the house would be prime hunting territory for the BGVs to disappear into. We obviously needed to fence in an area where they could run and play freely and safely; but we also needed to protect the local wildlife from this marauding bunch. We had started to research invisible fences that used ultrasonic or electric collars to contain dogs, but we were put off by reports that the hunting instinct in BGVBs was so strong that they would ignore the momentary pain the fence caused them if they caught a scent, thus rendering the border useless. However, we didn't want some ghastly metal eyesore enclosing our little piece of paradise and so when internet research revealed a different kind of 'invisible' fence we were delighted. We ordered one thousand feet of seven feet high black plastic deer fence that would enable us to enclose nearly two acres of our land. We were impressed by claims that from fifteen feet away it could not be seen, so we arranged that it would be delivered the day after my arrival in Canada.

Then we set about booking the dogs and cats in for their journey to the wilds. Fortunately Viv Phillips was able to recommend a company in London through whom she had shipped many of her dogs in years gone by. Sharon contacted them and we were most impressed with their caring approach. It was settled that they would collect the animals the day before shipping was due to begin. They would then be housed in their kennels. The only slight problem was that the carrier, Air Canada, who operated the only direct service to Calgary at that time, would only take two dogs on a flight at a time. Whilst our pack all had experience of going into kennels when we had been on holiday, we knew that they were stressed by the separation. For two, this kennelling would only be an overnight stay, for the others, more. Therefore we had to decide the order in which they would come; and so it was agreed that those who would be most stressed by being separated should come first. Dougal and Kaiti were nominated as the ones who would be the first to board the plane for the eight hour ride in the sky. Their flights would begin a week after I had arrived, giving me ample time to erect the fence. Sharon and the kids would follow two weeks later. Everything fell easily into place and the schedule fitted our needs perfectly.

Of course when I arrived, the fence did not. Every day I would be on the phone trying to track down its whereabouts and although some of it showed up at a FedEx depot near the airport, it was not the right bits to enable me to start putting it up. Finally, with only three days to go

98

before the arrival of the dogs, I was able to get the whole kit. The next morning I rose at 5.30am and began by building a small 'holding' area underneath the back deck that could be accessed from the basement family room. If all else failed, I could keep the dogs indoors and have them visit this area when they needed to go out. In addition to this and in anticipation of impending difficulties, I had bought four 30 foot long cable leashes that I attached to trees. If the BGVs were hooked onto these, they could be outside without me having to worry about them escaping and they could still move around a great deal. I didn't have to worry about the cats because they were too old to go anywhere and Kaiti and Pippa wouldn't wander off.

For the next two days I worked like a slave from dawn till dusk and by the time I came to leave for the airport to make the first collection, only 200 feet of the planned enclosure remained unfenced.

In the meantime Sharon had to cope with the heartbreak of handing the animals over to the shippers before they began their long journey. The agony of seeing them taken away, the sense of betrayal she imagined them feeling and their total lack of comprehension of what was happening is not a memory she likes to recall. Even for me, the anticipation of the animal's journey was a nightmare. I could well imagine their distress and I imagined their reaction to the flight itself with horror. However, it had to be done if we were to keep the family together and Viv reassured me that all would be well.

I was due to collect them from Calgary airport at a certain time but in my excitement to be reunited with them I got there 2 hours early. There was paperwork to sort out anyway and I had no idea of the procedure that I needed to go through in order to get them, so the time was not wasted. I discovered that the process was not complex but involved a lot of time and a great deal of movement between the airport and the cargo handling depot which was some distance away. Firstly I had to collect paperwork from the cargo handlers and then after the plane had landed I needed to go to the main terminal which was a 3km away. There I needed to park the car in short term parking, walk to the terminal, visit with the customs people to sign forms, get the cargo manifest signed off and pay the import charge. Then with all of these forms correctly completed I had to return to the car, pay for the parking on the way out, drive back to the cargo depot, present the forms and pay more fees before they would release the dogs who, in the meantime, had to undergo a veterinary inspection by a government vet which I also had to pay for.

I became progressively more and more anxious as time went by. The plane was late, the paperwork took forever and when I was finally led to the place to where the crated dogs awaited me, both looked as if they were heartbroken. Dougal wouldn't lift his head when called and had the predictably broken tail. Kaiti faced the solid rear wall of the crate and wouldn't turn round. And then as if by magic they both suddenly realised that it was me collecting them and joy broke out all around. I quickly loaded their crates onto the back of our rented pickup truck and drove a short distance to a patch of open land where I could let them out and we could have a proper reunion. They danced around and Kaiti did her chase the tail routine, her ultimate expression of excitement; whilst Dougal bayed in his rich hound's voice and tried to get his tail to function again. After that I didn't have the heart to put them back in the crates so they both rode the hour long journey back to the house in the cab of the truck, Dougal on the front seat beside me and Kaiti lying across the rear bench seat.

They greeted their new home with a total sense of acceptance as if they had known just what to expect. Kaiti in particular is very sensitive to new environments, and in the past, whenever we went somewhere new, she would be uncomfortable and stressed and would make herself a downright pain! Yet she adapted immediately and with no fuss whatsoever to her new home. It was as if she had an expectation of being where she now found herself and I have seldom seen her more laid back about anything. That night both dogs slept soundly. Since I had no bed as yet, they cuddled up next to me on the floor and I was very grateful for the company.

The next day I repeated the performance with marginally more ease. I took Dougal with me and he considered it his right to sit up in the front next to me. Today it was the turn of Emily, Daisy and the cats to arrive and the customs people seemed a little surprised to see me again, but they said nothing. However, a totally different scene met me at the cargo depot. The cats were making the most outrageous noises and

Emily was playing her confident flirt role with the cargo handlers, making eyes at anyone who would stop by to say hello. Daisy was none the worse for wear but a little more restrained. As soon as they saw me, they both began a cacophony of sound that, when combined with the cats yowling seemed to fill the vacuous cargo warehouse. Once again I did a hurried load, made the same stop of as the previous day (although I could not let Emily off the leash) and headed for home. Only the cats remained in their crates and it was interesting to observe the interactions between Dougal and the other dogs. He was undoubtedly pleased to see them but it was as if he was now the senior boy at school, confident in his knowledge of what everything was about, willing to share with them, but superior nonetheless.

Kaiti's greeting of them was a revelation in itself. Of all of our dogs, Kaiti always keeps herself to herself and is not really recognisable as a pack member. She accepts all and is accepted by all, but her interactions with the others are always on her terms and she will play only when she wants to play. However, her greeting of Emily and Daisy was one of frenzied pleasure and there was more than a faint suggestion that despite her stand-offish exterior, the pack was more important to her than we had previously believed.

That night I slept surrounded by dogs.

When it came to the third day and my third visit to customs, I was eyed with great suspicion and the guy on the desk announced that he needed to talk to his supervisor about all of these dog collections. After quite a long wait the supervisor returned and an interrogation began: Why was I bringing in these dogs? Was I a breeder? Was I going to sell the dogs? Was I bringing them in for somebody else? Why were there so many? My explanation that they were our pets didn't seem to impress the official and I began to get very worried that he wouldn't let Pippa and Molly into the country. Finally he said: 'I've looked at the paperwork and I can see how much it's cost you to bring all of these dogs over here. Why didn't you just buy new ones here instead? It would have been a lot cheaper." I was speechless and didn't know quite how to respond when one of his colleagues, a lady who had been sitting close by and apparently listening, came over and said quietly "Bob, you've never owned a dog have you?" He shook his head. "He's legit Bob. Let him in".

He nodded his acquiescence and thus our entire pack had officially arrived in Canada.

The journey home followed the now familiar pattern and Dougal repeated his old boy routine. The reunion of the six of them was a sight to behold and once again I was delighted to see Kaiti in the thick of it. Only the cats looked on with distain, clearly neutral at once again having to be part of a dog infested mad house!

The next week passed without too many incidents. The beds arrived and numerous other things we had ordered. Some I needed to collect but if ever I had to go out, Dougal insisted on coming with me. He now owned the front seat of the truck where he would sit proudly watching the road ahead. I dubbed him Truck Dog and his excitement with this new experience was palpable, as was his disappointment when the rental was eventually returned and we switched to a sedan. However, a couple of months later we took delivery of our own pickup truck, and we were to witness the return of the Truck Dog!

When I had only about eight feet of fencing left to put up. I was distracted by the arrival of our new neighbours who had come to say "hello". In a moment of carelessness I let the BGVs escape and they were through the open gap in the fence line like rats up a drainpipe. The smell of deer, elk, moose and lord knows what else must have been intoxicating. But it meant that the neighbours, who I learnt were called Scott and Shannon, met with a very tense and frustrated version of me who was none too keen on talking. But rather than dismiss me as an ignorant Brit, they simply joined in my pursuit of the dogs and after a blessedly brief period of time, we had them all safely rounded up. It was to be the first of many occasions on which they would lend their assistance with straying pack members.

The six dogs happily settled in our new house but the outside proved to be even more exciting with so many interesting sights, sounds and smells. In anticipation of what we might face in Canada from an environmental perspective, I had felt that it was important to acclimatise the dogs to some of the likely disruptions before they encountered them for real. First amongst these was the fact that we would live in the midst of coyote country and I knew from my brief experiences the previous fall that these wild dogs could howl all night long. So in the UK I had bought a CD of wolf cries and would put this on at random intervals. At first the dog's reaction had been one of immense disturbance. They prowled the room with wild eyes, rushed to the windows and barked in apparent fear. Sharon was appalled that I would do this to them but I persisted and they soon got used to the sound. After a matter of days, they registered no reaction whatsoever whenever I turned the CD on. A few days after they had all arrived and the fence was completed, we were visited by a coyote pack in the night. I was grateful that the fence was up and impenetrable as far as they were concerned, but they howled in very close proximity to the house. The noise was enough to wake me up and I was fascinated by this unearthly sound that was at once beautiful and eerily haunting. The dogs did not even stir and I am pleased to report that the howling of coyotes is something that they don't seem to think is real!

The downside of having coyotes nearby is that they have a thing about dogs: they like to eat them. They scent the area to attract the dogs, lure them away from their homes and then grab them. Locally this is a common phenomenon so we were pleased that our seven foot deer fence was more than a match for even the most determined coyote. Unfortunately almost as soon as the dogs arrived I started to notice that something was attacking the enclosure. At first I saw little holes start to appear and concluded that it must be the squirrels as they took great delight in loudly taunting the dogs. It was both amazing and hilarious to watch a squirrel run down a pine tree branch, paws stretched out in front quite deliberately pushing off all of the pine cones so that they fell onto the dogs heads below. Obviously we had blocked the easy access to 'their' land so they were making holes in retaliation. Feeling guilty, I cut holes at ground level every few yards for the entire fence boundary and felt confident that this would restore their happiness, and stop further attacks.

However, a few days later a very large hole appeared. I discovered it because Emily got through it and escaped. She was now totally free to roam over almost unlimited forested land with no way of being traced. Fortunately her hound's bay could be heard at least 2km away so I could tell quite easily where she was going. I tracked her for about an hour and finally intercepted her (much to her disgust) filthy and happy as a sand boy. Upon returning I immediately patched up the fence and took our precious cargo inside the safety of the house.

The following day all seemed to go well. I checked the fence line for holes again and it was all clear. But I noticed squirrels passing freely and easily through the existing fence and not through the man made holes I created. Clearly they were not our culprit. I spent a lot of time researching what might be eating the fence and concluded that it must be a wolverine or a porcupine. Then that evening Emily's manic barking alerted me to the fact that our mystery beast had struck again and Emily was gone.

This time it was dusk and the search became even more frantic. I chased her over our land and onto the Crown Land behind our property. It's worth mentioning that to get there you have to go through a swamp and over a small bridgeless river – not easy for a PBGV. Emily is a very determined little dog and I began to get worried about what was attracting her to the land. So it was with a mixture of horror and relief that after some time and in near darkness I heard unpleasant snarling sounds and Emily came tearing out of some undergrowth, practically leaping into my arms. Obviously she had found the coyotes and had a very lucky escape.

I needed to increase my vigilance on the fence since this creature, whatever it was, was not going to give up. I walked the fence line to check for holes before letting Emily out of the house. But on the third day, she escaped again, her close encounter obviously forgotten. Fortunately I was able to catch her after only 20 minutes. The fence was patched again.

Then a pattern set in: I patched; the animal attacked, Emily escaped; it was always after I'd checked the fence and allowed Emily the run of the perimeter. It went on for many days and Emily seemed to love it. Once she was out she'd let me get really close to her and suddenly she'd dart away. I developed search patterns and entrapment plans but all to no avail. She'd only come back when she was good and ready. She just didn't get that her life was at risk and I wanted to save her. I was nearly at my wits end. I didn't want to deprive her of her freedom within the fence line but I wanted her to be safe and I certainly didn't want Sharon to arrive and discover that her precious little dog had been eaten!

I gained an entirely new perspective on these events when, during an escorted tour of the land I watched with horror as I discovered what the animal was that was doing this to our fence and allowing our beloved pet to escape: It was a dog. A dangerous PBGV that bit holes in the fence solely for the purpose of gaining freedom. Right before my very eyes Emily expertly bit through the fence with the kind of skill and speed that only results from great practice. Only a scrambled dash enabled me to grab her back legs as they disappeared through the gaping hole she herself had created. Instantly Emily went under house arrest and was renamed Bin Laden: a terrorist always on the run! I had to go and buy one thousand feet of metal fencing and re-do the bottom of the fence line before it was safe to let her out again.

From Germany with love: Indy's tale – Part two

Sharon and the kids arrived two weeks after the pack. I collected them at the airport and of course, Dougal came with me. He was a little bit put out that Sharon took his front seat, but he was happy enough to sit between the children in the back as this meant a journey of being perpetually fussed with. When we got to the house it struck me that being reunited with the dogs was more exciting for everyone than seeing me! They all settled in very quickly but we only had two days to enjoy our new home together before I had to leave and fly to Frankfurt to collect our new avatar.

After a nine hour virtually sleepless flight I landed, collected a hire car and drove for over four hours to get to the kennels. I spent only an hour with Giselle before turning round and driving back the way I'd come, accompanied by Indiana Jones Vom Erlau, a very large and very scared puppy in a crate on the back seat. After less than 30 seconds in the car, he was overcome by stress and the interior instantly became intolerable. Somewhat embarrassed by the situation I waited until I was out of site of Giselle (who was still waving from her gate) before I pulled over and changed all of the bedding in his crate. After a repeat performance 3 minutes after starting off again, I put the crate on the front seat next to me, with the 'open' end facing me. This seemed to do the trick as his stomach was fine thereafter, but the crate kept pressing against the gear stick and changing it to neutral at the most inconvenient moments. Also, since I had driven the route that morning, elaborate preparations had been made for roadworks. The main highway to Frankfurt was closed and at the point where this occurred, there was a screen giving details of a detour. Unfortunately this was all in German and there was not one single sign afterwards. I had no road atlas and so I had to make up the rest of the journey with guesswork. It took six hours to get back to the airport. Fortunately we were checked in at a hotel across a walkway from the terminal and we passed a relatively peaceful night.

The next morning I faced the agony of handing Indy over to the baggage handlers. He cried pitifully and I was more upset than I would have believed possible. Because of all of the check in requirements, flight delays and unloading rigmarole, it was thirteen hours before I saw him again in Calgary and he was clearly very cross. I got him home as quickly as possible and we immediately gave him a bath, then he met the rest of the pack. Only Dougal wasn't too keen on welcoming another male and there exists between them to this day a strained relationship of tolerance rather than liking. Again, we were reminded that just because they are avatars, it doesn't mean that they recognise or like one another.

Jenny's response to Indy was the most interesting to observe. It would be fair to say that it was love at first sight and the feeling seemed to be reciprocated. They dance around together outside and she is able to teach him to do almost anything she desires. For his part, his favourite trick is to gently grip her arm in his jaws – with no pressure – and lead her wherever he wants her to go. However, she resists him sleeping in her room because his great hairy coat and mane mean that he gets hot very easily. It is not uncommon for him to want to get up and go out several times in the night, just to lie on the snow. Even the coldest of minus temperatures are meaningless to him and in the heat of summer, he has to sleep outside all night long.

Indy grew at an alarming rate. When he arrived with us he was bigger than Kaiti, Emily and Daisy, but within a couple of months only Pippa was taller. Such a big dog cut an intimidating figure when we took him out and about, but it quickly became apparent that size did not mean courage. Initially he was frightened of anybody new who came round. Gradually he progressed a little so that he accepted people, but he remained very scared of children. The smaller they were the more terrified he would become and the bigger he grew the worse it got. When he met someone, he would not look directly at them but around them with an odd intensity. We began to suspect that something was up.

There was an occasion when he was about 18 months old when I took him on a hike in a local beauty spot. It was winter and the snow was heavy on the ground. Indy was delighted to be out and about, particularly as we were the only ones around. We were due to do an 8km loop walk and had got about 3km away from the car when in the distance on the track ahead of us, we both spied a group of around sixteen senior ladies out enjoying the sun and snow. Indy froze and as they got closer, he refused to move an inch further. By now he weighed over 150 lbs and a dog that big is difficult to shift once his mind is made up; so I decided to wait it out until they had walked past us. Indy had other ideas and as they came closer he began to struggle to get out of his collar. Unfortunately I had not tightened it enough and he was able to slip out of it. He backed off one hundred metres, resisting my attempts to get him to return, then seeing that the oncoming of the old ladies was unstoppable, he turned tail and ran. When I finally caught up with him twenty minutes later, he was standing by the car trembling. Our walk was a long one that day.

His reaction to others was certainly unpredictable and whilst he was not aggressive beyond a little low growling, we felt the need to find some answers about what was going on with him. Michael was able to explain:

Indy was a very powerful avatar who had the ability to see energy fields. Whilst most dogs had an awareness of other's energies and emotions through their sense of smell, he was blessed (or from his perspective, perhaps cursed) with seeing them too. To him, people appeared much larger and more frightening than they were. Children were most scary of all.

What was Indy actually seeing?

Everyone is surrounded with an aura. This is an energy field that flows from within. It has depth and colour. Both change depending upon emotional state and circumstance. Auras can be huge and bright and extend a long way from the body but an adult burdened with concern may have a depleted aura. A child's is more likely to be strong and colourful.

When Indy sees any human being he sees their energy first and foremost. The reason he seemed to be looking so intently around or beyond people was because he was looking at their aura. This could be reasonably stable and flat or it could be very active and wild in appearance. He is often taken by surprise by the state of people's

---

energy fields since this is what he sees first. Since auras can change from meeting to meeting, he is also confused by the inconsistencies in what he sees.

Children are scary because their fields are so much bigger. Despite their small size, they would appear to him to be more daunting than most adults.

A more alarming incident came the following summer. We were taking a sixteen kilometre family hike that circumnavigated a gorgeous lake. It was a full day outing and we were about half way round when we were approach by a group of four teenage joggers running in a line. The first three passed without incident, but when Indy saw the forth, he made a lunge for her, snarling and baring his teeth. The poor girl was terrified and we were lucky that he was on a leash. If he had been off, I dread to think what might have happened. The prospect of this otherwise gentle and loving dog being put to sleep was too horrific for words. Nevertheless, we were deeply concerned about what had happened and immediately requested an explanation from Michael. Apparently the girl had some very 'heavy' energies attached to her. Indy's response had been to them and not the girl. In actual fact he had been trying to defend her.

What were the 'heavy energies?'

The girl had something in her energy field that was interfering with what a normal energy pattern should have looked like. Michael's response to my question was non-specific at the time but I have since come to understand that it was something that definitely should not have been there.

As we move about on a day to day basis it is only natural that our energy fields interact as they come into contact with one another. Often times we can pick up negative energies from another person who is having a bad day. They will attach to our field and interfere with it. They will eventually dissipate by themselves, or they can be cleansed.

110

In order to help Indy with what was clearly becoming a problem for him, we bought him a canine Q-Link which has the effect of damping electro-magnetic energies. This produced an almost immediate result, and he is now far more relaxed with what he sees.

Indy's arrival was to have more impact upon our household than we had previously understood. Whilst we had been told from the outset that he would be a powerful avatar, and we had come to learn that he had some energy issues, we never thought to ask about the cause or research any other implications; so we were a little bit taken aback at what started to happen next. To understand this, we need to go back a year:

The energy line

When I first came looking for houses in Alberta, I was given a map of the area. On it I plotted the locations of all of the houses that I was due to see and was surprised to note that you could draw a straight line that almost intersected all but two of them, with precious little deviation on either side. At the far north west point was a house with the most spectacular views that was totally unaffordable. Nevertheless the realtor took me to view the property as if guided to do so. After some very enjoyable discussions with the owners, they revealed that their land had an energy vortex on it and they invited me to go outside and experience it. Sure enough, about one hundred metres from the house I experienced a very intense encounter with some very palpable energy that swirled around a particular area forming a circle or cylinder. However, there was an off shoot of energy that proceeded in a south easterly direction.

I thought nothing more of this until I looked at my crudely drawn map again and realised that the off-shoot from the vortex seemed to run in parallel with the line of houses that I was viewing. What a strange coincidence I thought for a second, until it occurred to me that the vortex might actually be the start of an energy or ley line that even scientists acknowledge the existence of. And Michael quickly confirmed that it was indeed the start of the line. Even more intriguingly he explained that the reason so many properties were on the market along the line was because if the energies of those who lived there were not compatible with those of the line, they would be 'moved on'. Looking back I find it intriguing that once again, I thought no more of this. We bought our house and found ourselves living less than two hundred metres from the line. It ran through a field on the opposite side of the highway we live on and it never occurred to us to even ask if there would be any downside to this.

Shortly after we arrived we went to the opposite side of the road and had great fun walking towards the line. Sharon's energy healing work makes her unusually receptive to energies and the line presented her with an interesting new experience. We found that by the time you got within 10 metres of the line, you could begin to get a sense that there was something there. At five metres your whole body started to tingle. By the time you got to within a couple of metres, even your ears were buzzing with the sensation. If it was contained within the earth, it certainly didn't stay there. It seemed to rise up out of the ground and become all pervasive. It wasn't like the kind of static energy you can experience in an electric storm. It had a sense of power and depth about it, so much so that you almost expected to see it.

Having made the assumption that our energy line was of the common or garden ley variety, we thought that it would remain exactly where it was and that it was not a factor of consideration for us. So it was to our great surprise when Sharon began to experience some form of major shift in her sensing of the line. Specifically, she could experience the energy much more closely than she had before. Was it expanding we wondered? A quick recce of the area suggested one of two things: either the line was indeed getting wider; or it was moving.

Needless to say, a channelling session followed in which we asked what was going on. Michael confirmed that the line was on the move. Apparently it had been quite fixed in its previous location, but now it was being attracted by the energies emanating from our house and thus was moving towards us. We put forward our assumptions about the static nature of ley lines and were a little thrown by the answer: "It is not a ley line. It marks the perimeter of a merkaba which in turn represents the boundary of a designated Light City."

What is a merkaba? What is a Light City?

A merkaba is a three dimensional Star of David, or if you prefer, a star tetrahedron. It is known as a piece of 'sacred geometry' and if you look it up on Wikipedia (where it is spelt merkabah) you will discover that there is great significance attached to it in the Bible and in the Jewish faith.

Michael's explanation of the origins and purpose of a Light City was an evolving one that actually developed in its fullness over a period of two years. However, in highly abridged form it is an area marked by a merkaba that receives energetic infusions. The earth itself as a living

---

entity is constantly impacted by the somewhat parasitic activities of the human race. It is able to receive healing energies that are best described as 'cosmic' in their origins through particular areas on the planet. There are many of these. Some are termed 'light portals' and others light cities.

The designated Light City that we now lived on the edge of had always been there and had been dormant. However, due to the needs for energetic infusion at that time, the line had become active again a few years before our arrival and was gaining in strength, hence its effect upon those living on or near to it. It was coming towards our house at a very slow rate, but nonetheless it was getting closer. Right now it was just moving up to the highway.

It goes without saying that we were curious as to why it should be on the move. Michael explained: our presence in the house had caused a shift!

We were rather flattered that it found our energies appealing enough to be drawn to, but the angelic host seemed to find this little conceit quite amusing. Gently it was explained to us that it was not attracted to us at all; it was the avatars that were drawing it our way. Their powerful angelic energies not only acted as a magnet, they also amplified the line's own energy and caused an effect similar to that of a step-up transformer in an electric circuit. It was a wholly natural phenomenon and from the Light City's perspective, a highly desirable one since it enabled it to be much more effective.

This was easy enough to understand but we were thrown into confusion when Michael revealed that since we now had three avatars, their energy output was sufficient to cause this. The bit that confused us was the mention of the three avatars, so we did a quick count: Dougal and Indy. Only two! "You have not included the wisest and most powerful of the avatars" came the reply.

Another avatar

It wasn't really a surprise to learn that Kaiti was also an avatar. She always had a guru like quality about her and her aloofness only added to her appearance of being some kind of Zen master. What wasn't so clear was what her purpose with us had been. We were reminded that all of what had now come to pass had begun with Kaiti. Without her presence in our home we would never even have entertained the idea of having more dogs. She had been responsible for opening up what was described as our 'circle of love'.

A circle of love

The emotion of love carries with it a powerful vibration that supports harmonic resonance of the most positive vibrations of the earth. It is totally synergistic with our purposes, whatever they may be, and it adds value to not only our personal state of wellbeing but that of the collective consciousness. We experience it when we are loved; we emit it when we love. The more love we receive the more we imbibe of that which is for our own highest good. The more love we put out the more we service the highest good of all. A 'circle of love' is effectively created by the loving relationships that exist in close proximity to one another. Hopefully, many households have them. The contribution made to the circle is created by the emotions of all those who are within the proximity and yes, animals certainly do have emotions and they can certainly contribute.

So by having a household with eight dogs, two cats and two children, we were starting to develop a mighty powerful circle of love.

The sheer magnitude of the task that she was to perform required that she bring in an immense amount of light with her because the effect that she brought about was to transmute our beliefs and values and cause a cascade of wholesale change within our lives. She was described as the most powerful of the avatars because of this energy. Whilst her influence would appear to have been a passive one this was far from the case. That which Sharon had so often jokingly described as Kaiti's Shar

117

Pei mind tricks' was far closer to the truth than she could have imagined. Her presence had actually had a mind altering impact.

How could Kaiti affect our thinking?

A thought that is conceived within the mind creates a vibration. Whilst the words that give voice to the thought may directly reflect, add to or alter that vibration, even if it is not spoken, the vibration is still transmitted. It may be described as a thought wave. Because we have forgotten how to receive communication in this way, most of us are unable to receive thought waves in a way that allows us to *intentionally* interpret them. If we can, it is called telepathy.

Dogs are able to both transmit and receive information telepathically by choice and intent. This is how Kaiti was able to communicate with us. We would have been largely unaware of this as it would have been subtle. Her thought waves would have filtered into our consciousness when we were least aware of it; we would need to be relaxed, open and not otherwise focused. The vibrations she put out would have been suggestive of a course of action and highly appealing.

The inevitable question of how we could understand her arises. This is not even an issue of her being an avatar:

At the instant at which a thought is conceived, it has no language. It is transmitted without being enveloped in the specific spoken language that we use to give it voice. Therefore telepathy requires no understanding or knowledge in order for it to be interpreted. It is a universal communicator in the truest sense of the term.

Perhaps you have encountered animal communicators? They are individuals who are sensitive enough to these thought vibrations to be able to pick up on them. The understanding is a foregone conclusion if the individual accepts that it is 'real' and is able to get past their belief that they are not simply hearing themselves and their incessant internal chatter. However, it should be noted that this ability is very like channelling and relates to level of vibration.

118

To perform her task Kaiti needed to be fully conscious of her purpose from the outset. From the perspective of the angelic realms (as will become apparent later in the book), her purpose in kick starting our circle of love was too great to be something that she would only come upon later in her life. Therefore she incarnated with full knowledge of that which she truly was and what she was to do. This is why she was described to us as the wisest avatar. Of all of them, she was and still remains the only one with full knowledge of what she is.

A long awaited return: Peri's tale

In October of 2006 I went to spend 3 weeks in Berlin, something I had done on several occasions before we moved to Canada. I stayed in a small and now very familiar hotel just off Kurfurstendamm, delivering very intense five day cycles of something I call 'hothouse coaching' to small groups who flew in at the weekends. We worked until 5pm each evening but then I was free until the next morning and I also had the weekends to myself. I figured that the groups would have had enough of me during the day, so I never accompanied them in the evening when they went out to eat. Instead I walked many kilometres around the city, saw at least one or two operas on every visit and got to know Berlin quite well.

Wandering around a city by yourself can be a pretty lonely experience when you don't have anyone to share it with. It becomes doubly so when you are isolated by the language barrier, and since, to my eternal shame, I don't speak anything but English, these trips could have been pretty depressing. However, I managed to fill the time and enjoyed the freedom of total anonymity and the peace and quiet of self reflection that followed days when I had been doing a great deal of talking.

This trip was to be my last in the cycle of programs I was running for the client. It was all about influencing skills and I began the week by covering my patented influencing techniques model. I then had the participants spend the rest of the week perfecting the skills learnt by applying them to situations where influence was required. It should have been a straightforward series of classes much as the previous sessions had been. I arrived from Canada via England on Saturday, and spent the weekend getting over the jetlag, walking the parks and streets. And then I was overcome by the rather strange experience of seeing Poodles everywhere.

I would turn on the television and there would be a programme about dogs, featuring Poodles. If I switched channels there might be a drama with a Poodle in the scene. If there was a movie, it was as if it was obligatory to have a Poodle in it. But if I went outside, I couldn't help but see a person walking a Poodle. If I went to an art gallery, there would be pictures of Poodles. A bookstore seemed to have Poodle books featured. In clothes stores I saw sweatshirts with Poodle silhouettes on them. The sheer abundance of Poodles was not only outrageous, it was downright annoying.

At this point, in case you haven't already guessed, I should confess that despite my grandmother having owned one, I am very definitely not a fan of Poodles. There is something about their form and temperament that annoyed me intensely. I found them ugly and froufrou. Of course these judgements were quite unkind and with precious little foundation. My experience with Peri had only ever been positive.

The Poodle glut reminded me of Gran and her love affair with Peri. Such a memory being sparked may not be so unusual, but what I did next probably is: I used her situation following Peri's death as a case study. Following the presentation of the influencing techniques model I outlined to the group the story of what had befallen my grandmother, omitting to mention any personal facts or reveal that it was actually a true story. Then across the course of the week, I had them employ the various stratagems they learned to this situation to see if they could persuade the 'old lady' to get a new dog. I played Gran's part in the role plays, responding as she had done in life. Perhaps I was trying to alleviate my own feelings of regret and guilt. Perhaps I was looking to see if there was anything that could have been done to change her mind. Whatever, across the three weeks and fifteen trainees, nobody managed to produce an argument compelling enough to change 'her' mind.

In the meantime, the Poodle presence in Berlin in all forms was becoming rampant and, somewhat slow on the uptake, I started to feel that something strange was happening. I confided in one of the participants to test if he had noticed this strange phenomenon. He looked at me in a very puzzled way and replied that he hadn't noticed a single one.

In the third and final week I walked down to the famous German department store Ka De We. I was wandering aimlessly through the store, going from floor to floor on the escalators admiring the fine displays and abundance of products. I happened to notice the signs that were at the entrance to each flight of the escalator prohibiting taking dogs on the moving staircase. Instead of the usual non-descript dog one sees depicted in these signs, the ones in Ka De We quite clearly pictured a Poodle! I was stunned and then suddenly I started to hear Michael's voice in my head and realised that he had been trying to get my attention for three weeks.

I tuned in and he said: "There's an angel here that wants to speak to you". The effect was like the burst of a dam in my mind. For a second I had a blinding glimpse of clarity and knowledge of what was to come and for the sake of clarity, I left the store.

Why I didn't listen to Michael

When you are an open channel, you can hear 'stuff' all of the time so there is a need to develop an internal on/off switch. An open channel can hear communications from any entity that has the inclination to communicate with them and this includes angels, ascended masters, elementals and nature devas (ancient spirits responsible for different aspects of being in the world of nature). I once had the curious experience of conversing with a rock deva at Moraine Lake in Alberta for two hours. Nobody had spoken to it in over two thousand years so it had a lot to say! Eventually I had to tell it "I have to go now" and I hurried away, only to be intercepted by a tree deva that was equally garrulous. After that I learned to turn off pretty quickly!

The angelic realms don't mind you switching off. They acknowledge the pressures of third dimensional living and are grateful for the time that you will allow them. But that doesn't mean to say that it is always alright to turn off.

In Berlin, as always, I was very used to channelling my higher self so as to deliver what my client wanted from me. Whilst this required me to be constantly open, the traffic of communication became filtered by my needs rather than theirs and nothing that did not correspond with my immediate needs came through. I allowed nothing that was a distraction.

Thus, whilst Michael was trying to speak to me, I was ignoring him.

Therefore very elaborate means were used to get my attention. It does not surprise me one iota that others would not have experienced the 'Poodle glut' that filled my consciousness. I believe that it probably only featured in my individual reality. But I know now that it happened because I wasn't listening, which was in turn, my choice.

I still make that mistake sometimes. I block what I don't particularly want to hear; I refuse to acknowledge messages that I am asked to relay; I deny the reality of what I experience; sometimes I even distort the messages that are given to me because I believe that they are too powerful to relay or because they mismatch with my needs.

Slowly but surely I am realising that the words of wisdom that are gifted to me are never wrong and that the cost of ignoring them is mine and mine alone. The privilege of hearing such things should not be underestimated.

The next few minutes were a revelation in many ways as Michael began to explain both the events of the past three weeks and relay the message for the angel: This particular angel had already lived a lifetime on earth as an avatar. It had come to help assuage the pain of a lady whose husband had died under terrible circumstances and it had come to stop the flood of grief and anger that had resulted. It had been successful in its mission and had lived a happy life in partnership with its human. It had died aged 15 and had not been on the earthly plane for over 25 years. It had sought permission to revisit now and wondered if we would consider taking it into our home. It had embodied as a dog. Specifically, it had been a Poodle and would come back as one again.

I was moved, but extremely reluctant. Through Michael I expressed gratitude for the fact that it had requested to come into our home and relayed that I felt honoured. However, we already had seven dogs and my wife wouldn't consider another. In my dialogue I tried not to call to mind that neither of us even liked Poodles but it knew anyway. It was quite persistent and gave commitments that it would be accommodating and good natured but still I resisted. I began to get more entrenched in my opposition and started to close down the conversation.

Then Michael said "When this being was here before its name was Peri". I caught my breath and the floodgates of emotion opened. I wept openly and moved off the brightly Kurfurstendamm into the shadows of the backstreets. Gently he explained that this was the same avatar that had lived with Gran and that most unusually it had been granted permission to have a second incarnation in the third dimension. But it could only come if we would accept it, and bearing in mind, as always, that we had freedom of choice, we could most certainly refuse.

What could I say? Well, unbelievably, I didn't cave in. I promised that I would give the matter some consideration and decided that maybe it was all just a reaction to the Poodle glut. Perhaps I was becoming unusually fanciful and the powerful emotions of revisiting Gran's plight through the case study had caused this strange effect within me.

Why the angel couldn't speak to me directly

You might be wondering at this point why the angel hadn't spoken to me itself?

Surely that would have made the case more compelling?

In actual fact it could have done, but I wouldn't have been able to hear it.

This is because within the hierarchy of angels, (which is an issue of role, not one of seniority or status, as these things are of no consequence to them) angels have a frequency of vibration that is of a much lower level than that of archangels. This makes them closer to human beings and allows for a greater degree of empathy with our experience. It also means that they are more aware of our needs and they are much better positioned to offer support in all manner of ways, which is after all, their role.

It also makes them more easily accessible for communication if the human is able to make the relatively small step of raising their vibration to that of the angel.

An archangel's vibration however, is considerably higher. In order to get to the point where I could successfully channel archangels I had to raise my vibration to their level and in so doing, I can no longer hear angels with a lower vibration.

Anybody can channel if they are willing to do so. Most people do get angelic communication at some point in their lifetime, but they are receiving communication from their guardian angel whose vibration, of all those entities in the angelic realms, is closest to their own.

A guardian angel is not just with you for life, but for all of your lifetimes. They are intimately acquainted with you and the essence of your being which is often referred to as your higher self.

Their role is almost parental in nature, ensuring as much as possible your arrival at those key points in your life that you have agreed to before incarnating and your safe passage along your pathway when needs warrant.

In truth, I didn't give the angel the consideration I promised. I didn't even mention anything to Sharon when I called home.

The only direct result was that on the last day of that week when we were reviewing the case study and the failure of anyone to persuade the old lady to get another dog, I revealed for the first time that the 'story' was true and that it was really about my grandmother. I felt an overwhelming sense of sadness as I said it and I was very conscious of the tears in my eyes.

I'm not sure if anyone noticed.

A Poodle? You must be joking! : Briony's tale

After the classes finished in Berlin I flew to the UK to deliver another event and it was not until a further two weeks had passed that I returned home. I was greeted by a wildly enthusiastic pack of dogs and a family interested to know of all that I had experienced. I didn't reveal a single thing about the Poodle glut or the reasons behind it!

During this time I didn't hear from the avatar again so I decided to forget about it as an aberration in my channelling and I felt quite relieved that I wouldn't have to tell Sharon that we were invited to get yet another dog.

However, around two weeks after I'd returned home we had just finished dinner when Michael very clearly asked "When are you going to tell her about the avatar?" "I'm not" I replied. "It would be appropriate to tell her now" he said. "No" came my rather surly response. "Why do you choose to deny her the choice?" came back quick as a flash. The dialogue continued for a few minutes more with the usual pattern of cracked record being played with me saying "No" and him simply requesting that I "tell her now".

Finally, visibly squirming, I said to Sharon "I've got some bad news". By now she could recognise not only the tone but the look on my face. "It's another dog isn't it?" I explained everything that had happened in Berlin and she listened without comment until I mentioned that it was Gran's dog that wanted to return. Big tears rolled down her cheeks at the mention of her name. Sharon and Gran had been close friends. Despite an age difference of over sixty years they got on like a house on fire and I often said, without really joking, that Gran preferred Sharon to me. She had often talked to her about Peri and although Sharon had never actually met the dog, she had a very strong sense of the closeness of the bond between them. When faced with such a plaintiff request from this particular source, she acceded immediately.

However, Sharon's feelings about Poodles were, if anything, stronger than my own. The idea of actually owning one was abhorrent, so as an opening gambit she asked if the avatar would come back as another breed. There then followed fifteen minutes of what was one of the most bizarre experiences I'd had of channelling. Basically it consisted of a four way negotiation between Michael, the avatar, Sharon and I.

Imagine the scene: two forty something adults sitting in front of the fire place. There's nobody else in the room and we're having a conversation which, from an observers perspective seems to be between ourselves. I say something or Sharon says something then after a few seconds, I relay what another party, who doesn't appear to be there, has told me another party has told them, who also doesn't appear to be there either. It must have been comical to say the least!

I have taught negotiation skills and from a third dimensional perspective, I'm not half bad at it, so I quite fancied our chances. We began by attempting to persuade the avatar to change breeds, offering a range of what we considered to be suitable (i.e. acceptable to us) range of alternatives, pointing out their finer qualities. For its part, the avatar countered with commitments of its temperament, loyalty and affection. It promised to be the easiest dog to live with, to get on with the other dogs, to be clean and to cause us no trouble. In fact it was extremely generous in its offerings. But it would not budge one inch on breed. Even when I said it plain, loud and straight out: "But we don't like Poodles" it simply replied "I will be a Poodle".

So in the face of overwhelming stubbornness, I did what all negotiators do as a final option and said that we would withdraw completely. A long and empty silence followed. "What's happening" asked Sharon? "I guess it's thinking about it" I replied, quite pleased with the impact of my ploy. But my smugness was soon shattered when Michael volunteered: "Don't forget it's an angel. It knows you don't mean it." It suddenly dawned on me that we were negotiating with odds overwhelmingly stacked against us.

So after a very brief discussion we both agreed that we could accept a Poodle but we would need to get into the issue of colour and size. Neither of us wanted a miniature Poodle (as Peri had previously been) and we absolutely could not consider a toy, if only for fear of how the other dogs, the majority of whom were hunting hounds, would react to such a tiny creature. And Peri's previous colour, blue, which is kind of

128

mid grey, not quite silver, not quite charcoal, was also unacceptable. In fact we didn't want grey of any shade, so after a quick conference with Sharon we proposed chocolate or apricot. Apparently these demands presented no problem for the avatar. It was prepared to be bigger and it would be chocolate it said. We're getting somewhere, strike one up for us! "And I'm going to come back as a female again and I want to be called "Briony" it said. We sat looking at each other in dumb surprise but both said simultaneously "That's fine".

Our 'negotiation' was pretty much of a walk over with the avatar getting everything it wanted. But we didn't feel that we had lost out. It just remained for us to discover how we were going to get it. And even here, it seemed to have things all planned out. I was instructed to go to the computer and access a certain website. On the website I was told that I would find a breeder who had an upcoming litter and that I would be able to reserve a puppy. It would be convenient and a process without complication or difficulty. The avatar would enter the body of the puppy at birth but the breeder would allow us to choose the puppy and we would be guided as to which one to select. The final thing it said was "Please tell your father I'm looking forward to seeing him again".

Sure enough, I went to the computer and within seconds had found the site with details of the upcoming litter, just as the avatar had said. I was able to put our name down on a waiting list and the puppies were due around Christmas. From Michael's reminder to having signed up, it all happened within the space of two hours. Now all we had to do was come to terms with the humiliation of owning such a froufrou creature!

Why was Peri allowed to come back?

The average pet on its ascension pathway has to reincarnate again and again in order to fulfil its objectives and ascend. But if an angel incarnates as an avatar, it's a one hit thing.

There are many more angels than there are humans. They are allocated to humans either on a specific or floating basis (a bit like being members of an angelic pool). As already explained, they do not envy what we go through but they do harbour desire to understand our experience with a

129

greater degree of empathy. To this end there is always a queue to experience avatar living as there are many more volunteers than there are available opportunities. Thus, if selected, the often unbearably brief experience of avatar living cannot be repeated because of the sheer volume of numbers who also await this privilege.

What I didn't really 'get' at this point was just how special her return therefore was, or why she had been allowed to return at all? When we asked Michael we received a vague explanation of unfinished business with me and also a rare glimpse into the interactions that take place in post-life review before transitioning into the next incarnation:

Everyone is able to be reunited with those animals that have been part of their lives if they so choose because of the synergistic learning purposes that form those bonds in the first place. They form an intrinsic part of our earthbound experience and we of theirs. They take a recognisable form but at this point we are able to communicate with them in the fullest manner possible. It is a sad mistake to believe that we are more than them, even whilst we are on earth together.

The angel that incarnated as Peri had been reunited with my grandmother upon her death. They met as equals. It is only our somewhat mistaken reverence for angels that makes us feel that they are above us. From their perspective, we are all the same, because ultimately, we are.

They reviewed all that they were meant to, and Gran had most certainly discussed the nature of her relationship with Sharon and the nature of Sharon's role in the wider scheme of things. This much we know.

But why was Peri allowed to come back?

Sharon likes to believe that Peri came back just so that she could experience a lifetime with her. But there's probably a little more to it than that! As I write this, the return of this avatar is still a mystery to me. I know the purposes of all of our avatars *except* Briony. I don't know why she received this dispensation. All I do know is that it is *very* rare. We are told things when the time is right for us to know them.

Sometimes it can feel a little like the wool is being pulled over your eyes and the truth comes out as if by drip feed (as stories yet to come will amply illustrate). So we have learnt to trust that everything is for our highest good and the highest good of all. And so it is!

That night I wrote an email to my father explaining what had come to pass. Since he of all family members had known Peri best, I thought that he was entitled to hear she was coming back. I thought about having a telephone conversation to explain but I still felt very emotional about the whole thing and couldn't risk breaking down as I told him. Even the note I wrote took some doing and the tears fell as I told him the joyous, if somewhat odd, news. I tried to make it as matter of fact as possible and I removed all of the sentiment that was associated with it. I wish I still had the email to include it in this book. Alas, it has been deleted. However, I do remember his reply: "That's interesting!"

The next day we broke the news to the kids, only to be met with cries of derision at our choice of pet and out-and-out horror that we would get such an embarrassing dog. Jenny in particular considered that it would be an affront to her sense of 'cool' to admit to her friends that she shared her home with such a thing. A friend in the UK had shared her home with a particularly annoying Poodle that her been her mother's froufrou pet and it had been silly and yappy. So why hadn't we made it come back as something else? Why had we given in? Why did we allow it at all? In fairness they were both too young to have really experienced a relationship with Gran and they couldn't appreciate the emotional imperative that Sharon and I felt. And they hadn't even known that Peri existed. So why should they care that (as Jenny put it) "some random avatar wanted to invade our lives"?

The weeks passed quickly with precious little enthusiasm from the kids, although Sharon and I began to warm to the idea of the incoming angel. The puppies were born just after Christmas and when they were old enough to be distinguished between, the breeder sent us photographs. Peri/Briony was obvious and Michael confirmed my recognition. I replied by email that she was the one we wanted. An avatar that had not walked the earth for twenty five years was on its way back to join an at least partially familiar family.

131

As the time of her arrival got closer the anticipation was a curious mixture of excitement and trepidation. We told Scott and Shannon all that had happened and after they got past the incredulity with the idea that such things were even possible, we faced the inevitable torrent of teasing and good natured abuse about pom pom tails, pink rinses and diamond studded collars. In fact anyone we told seemed to think that Poodles were the most dreadful dogs on the planet and although we certainly did not regret our decision, we may have thought "Oh dear..." on more than one occasion.

I have often wondered what the breeder would have thought had she known our reasoning behind coming to her and the true nature of what it was she was letting go of. Would anybody part with an angel if they knew they had one? Of course it's not really the sort of thing you open with when you're dealing with a complete stranger although there was a part of me that really wanted to tell her the whole tale. However, in February Briony was consigned to the cargo hold of a plane on Vancouver Island and made the one hour flight to our local airport.

I was in the US at the time so I missed her arrival. Having had the experience of collecting our UK pack and then flying with Indy from Germany, I was much more relaxed about the whole process by now. But for Sharon and Jenny awaiting an in-transit dog was a first and I can empathise with how they must have felt. Fears of Poodle ownership had by now disappeared to be replaced by total concern for the wellbeing of an eight week old puppy torn away from its home, its siblings and all that was familiar to it. Having previously received five puppies into our home already, we were all too familiar with the obvious angst the tiny creatures go through. Sharon and Jenny could well imagine the stress and heartbreak Briony would be feeling and knew that they would be collecting a very sad and frightened little being.

Get real.

Briony arrived as a bundle of pure love and confidence. She seemed to be overwhelmed by the sheer pleasure of meeting Sharon and as pleased as if she had been reunited with a long lost best friend. The only emotions she demonstrated were happiness and excitement. During the drive back home she sat on Jenny's lap barely able to contain her exhilaration. Ten minutes into the journey she had won the heart of what was probably her sternest opposition. Five minutes after her arrival at the house, she'd conquered Tristan's too, greeting him like a much loved brother. She treated the rest of the pack as if they were already known to her and slept that first crucial night as soundly as a bell. The only thing that Sharon could report to the breeder when she rang to confirm the puppy's safe arrival was that she seemed to be absolutely delighted to be in our home. Although the breeder was clearly relieved that all was well, Sharon even felt a little guilty that the transition from home to home was marked by a total absence of any apparent remorse or feelings of displacement.

When I arrived home a few days later, the Poodle already owned my house. She was doted upon by everyone and although Scott and Shannon were still less than enthusiastic, she had certainly captured the hearts of everyone else. It took about four minutes before I too melted all of my previous prejudices. She was not only delightful, she was also everything that the angel had promised her avatar self would be, and more.

That night I channelled Michael and we realised what should have become apparent eight weeks previously: now that the avatar was in its earthbound form, we could no longer speak to it. It is perhaps a little odd, but certainly true to say that it was quite a sad experience to receive this knowledge. Despite the fact that it had arrived safely in our home and we had another angel in our midst, it had returned to a state of ignorance of what it was, utterly dependent upon us and disarmingly at our mercy. The mighty being with which we had attempted to negotiate was now wholly subject to our auspices. It was both humbling and awing. A feeling of the sheer responsibility of owning an avatar came clearly into focus for the first time. And so did the realisation that not all those avatars who venture into our dimensions are received with quite the same loving kindness that we would lavish upon our pets.

Avatar preferences

I was not really surprised when at one point Michael explained that avatars prefer to go to households where they know that they will be safe, loved and secure.

In large part this is due to the fact that their vibration is much higher than that of the average non-avatar dog. This means that they are much more sensitive to the energies around them. The experience is far more difficult to cope with if the energies of a household are denser and contain emotions such as intense anger.

They also do not wish to find themselves in a situation where the essential dog nature of the being they have occupied does not allow their angelic selves to come to the fore. Yet the animal instinct which is part of the physical DNA is always present and has to be overcome. If the angel does not master its avatar form or ever arrive at the reawakening to what it really is, it can fail in its task. Angelic beings are not infallible. In third dimensional form they are every bit as vulnerable as we are.

Yet despite this, many will still volunteer to go through great hardships just for the sake of helping humans to become reconciled with their learning experiences. They will knowingly enter homes where there is violence and hardship for them just so that they may offer the opportunity for development to their owners.

For some, the ultimate result of their incarnations will be that they are cast aside when their service has been performed. A surprising number will find themselves experiencing the misery of dog pounds, humane societies or other refuges. They are just as subject as the average mutt to the nightmare experience of finding themselves being executed due to being unwanted.

The lot of the average puppy is the equivalent of being cast into the void. There is a massive degree of unpredictability about whom their owners will be and once they leave their mothers, their lives are utterly subject to the circumstances of their owners, who could be anyone.

It's a terrifying prospect and it is a testament to the benevolence of the essence of their being that they are prepared to undergo this trial on our behalf.

Briony rapidly became known as Brion, or to Scott and Shannon, 'the Poodle'. This sort of caught on and we regularly found ourselves calling her simply 'Poodle'. To this day, she is the only dog that we have that will look up or even come running in response to her breed name as well as her given name.

Even more curiously to an outsider, she will also give the same response if you call her Peri. It's not something she's called often, but occasionally I do it to see if the soul memory is still present. It always is and when I look deep into those gorgeous eyes of hers, I can still see Peri.

My dog is an avatar

If it ever struck my father as strange that his mother's dog was really an angel in disguise that reincarnated more than twenty five years after it died, to some people this was just perfectly normal. It was an odd phenomenon to experience, but the more we became involved with channelling, the more we seemed to attract people who were fully conversant with the concepts and language that Michael et al had been revealing.

On the one hand this was excellent because it gave the opportunity to discuss these ideas freely and openly without fear that someone was going to think me an idiot. On the other, it began to bring us into contact with some quite unusual people.

We met many wonderful individuals who were charming and very well intended; there were also encounters with people who struck me as *very* strange and over the top. There was a disconnected air about them as if they were somehow intentionally divorcing themselves from reality in their efforts to become higher dimensional beings. Sometimes it was embarrassing, sometimes just plain funny. I have met so many reincarnations of Cleopatra that I have lost count.

Funnily enough, it never occurred to me that from another perspective I might appear to be every bit as strange as them, at least in some of the things I now absolutely believed to be true. I still felt perfectly normal and if I never happened to mention it (and believe me, it's not the sort of thing you drop casually into a conversation) you would never know that I channelled.

It was and still remains the case that my delivery of any information that I have is totally matter of fact. Although I do not lack sensitivity, I am well aware that I often fall short of the desire of others for there to be an otherworldly quality about me. There simply isn't. Some people also expect that because of my own beliefs, I will instantaneously and automatically accept any claims they may make about spiritual matters. Unfortunately I will *only* believe what Michael or one of the beings I channel tells me is true.

Through a friend for whom I had channelled we were approached by a lady who asked if I would do a private channelling for her and we arranged to visit her at her house the next week.

When we arrived at the lady's house she welcomed us at the door and immediately invited us to follow her as there was something that she wanted to show us. She led us through to a room at the back of the house where a rather corpulent dog was sleeping soundly, evidenced by the volume of the snoring he emitted. She gazed upon the dog fondly and announced to us with a great deal of pride: "This is my dog Randy. He's an avatar".

"No, he's not" said Michael loud and clear in my head as the lady looked to me for affirmation. I smiled uncomfortably and managed to say "Oh, right..."

I seldom remember anything clearly from a channelling session so when, an hour later, I 'emerged' from my out of body state, I was surprised to discover that the lady was clearly a little put out. Sharon was bravely trying to explain a point to the lady who was quite teary and irritated. "What's going on?" I asked, hoping that I was misinterpreting the scene that was unfolding before me.

It transpired that the lady had asked what the avatar's purpose had been in coming to live its lifetime with her. Michael had simply answered "The dog is not an avatar" but the response was unacceptable to her. "It is!" she countered. "The dog is not an avatar" Michael repeated. A long and tense silence had followed before she had decided to change the subject and resume her questioning.

She might not have been prepared to argue for too long with an Archangel, but she didn't mind arguing with me!

The basic tenet she followed was that the dog was saintly. It seemed to know her every thought and responded to them almost before they entered her mind. The dog had never been any trouble. Even as a puppy he had never made a mess, chewed anything, stolen any food or bitten anyone. He could be walked without a leash and he would never run off.

When he encountered other dogs, he had never had any conflict with them. If there were children in the house, he would let them do anything to him without so much as a grumble. If the lady went out and left the dog in the house, he would be waiting at the window for her to return. If ever there was somebody who had bad energy the dog would give a low growl to warn her. Once when she had accidentally left the gas on in the kitchen and she could not smell it because she had a bad cold, the dog had barked loudly and repeatedly run into the kitchen until she followed it and discovered her error.

The list of reasons to beatify the dog went on and on, in fact it seemed that the only thing he didn't do was make the coffee in the morning.

The evidence presented, she sat back, confident that she had made her case.

I had no doubt that this was a very wonderful dog, but that's about all it was: "I'm afraid that all of those things don't make Randy an avatar" I said. Total indignation very obviously welled within her so I moved quickly on to explain by answering the unasked question: If a dog that appears so angelic is not an avatar, what is it?

It's a dog and what's wrong with that?

It is ironic but a dog that seems to be angelic is actually quite unlikely to be an avatar. When an animal behaves in a fashion similar to that described by the lady, it is far more likely that it is 'in balance'.

What is being 'in balance'?

It is a common feature of the learning requirements of many beings that exist on earth that they need, as their ultimate aim, to achieve balance. (In fact I now teach classes for humans who wish to understand what this means and how to do it.)

Basically, as we go through multiple lifetimes, we experience polarity and as part of this we do good and bad in different incarnations. But as we progress and learn, the emphasis in our learning moves from the need to merely experience life, through to the need to exercise choice within our life so as to balance our experience in favour of what is appropriate. This doesn't mean being perfect. It means being balanced!

It's pretty much the same thing for dogs. Although it is difficult for us to conceive of the way in which this could be played out, it has a lot to do with those elements that would form the features of a dog's life. For example, a balanced dog would be neither timid nor aggressive. It would exist in synergy with the needs of its humans neither being too dependent nor too independent. It would be loving but not needy.

Many factors of behaviour would feature as well as other influences that are not readily apparent to us such as the nature of their relationships with other dogs and creatures around them.

As we do good and bad across our lifetimes, so do dogs. As they learn they progress in soul levels until they reach the ultimate goal of achieving balance; and then they are able to move on in their development as spiritual entities.

Like humans, animals are on the ascension pathway. Their route is somewhat different from ours and contrary to some belief systems, there is no cross-over. However, they are pursuing the same purpose as us: Across a number of lifetimes they need to experience the polarities of the parameters of the possible through the range of their experiences; and they need to achieve balance through choice. Like us too, they go through phases of soul development. An animal that seems to be angelic is, on the balance of probability, more likely to be an old soul coming into balance than an avatar.

The equanimity achieved by an old soul is likely to be far greater than that attained by an avatar that is having its first third dimensional experience that may, for many reasons, be proving to be a real struggle.

After I had relayed these counter arguments the lady regarded me with a disdainful look and said: "Well, whatever you say, I know my dog is an avatar."

We withdrew without further comment and perhaps needless to say, we have never heard from her since.

A brief encounter

It was now a full year since I had the manic Poodle experience in Berlin and life was returning to normal. Our eight dog, four avatar pack was getting along nicely and I was confident that there would be no further growth. Michael had been quite quiet on the subject of canines since the 'negotiation', so all was well. In October I was in the UK for a few weeks running more courses and I missed the dogs terribly; so it was with eager anticipation that I arrived back at the airport and was greeted by Sharon who had come to collect me.

We drove along in beautiful sunshine discussing the events of our separate past few weeks. After some time Sharon went quiet. I thought nothing of the pause until with a voice that registered some discomfort she said: "You know when you left there were eight dogs?" I knew what was coming: "Well, at the moment there are nine."

I wasn't fazed at all. In fact I was actually rather pleased. But a quick word from Michael recommended that I remain neutral. Sharon went on to explain the circumstances:

During my time away there had been a cattle drive past our house. Apparently at some point during the drive a Husky had 'attached' itself to the herd. Upon arrival, the ranch owner had angrily told a farm hand to take the dog back to where it had come from. Of course he didn't know where it had joined up, so he went back down the highway and the first home he had been able to gain access to was Scott and Shannon's. Asking them if they could solve the mystery of its ownership, he was told that their next door neighbours had dogs, but that it definitely wasn't one of theirs.

Very shortly thereafter Tristan found the dog deposited at our gate and was just in time to see the farmhand walking away.

Naturally, the dog was welcomed with open arms and happily took up residence in our house. In the meantime Sharon contacted local vet's surgeries and humane societies in an effort to find the dog's real owner. She put up a lost sign at the post office and posted an ad on an internet lost/found dog site; but all was to no avail. The only response she had was from a broken hearted man who'd lost an Alaskan Malamute. He was hoping that a mistake might have been made in breed identification; but it was not to be.

So I arrived home to be greeted by the usual enthusiastic mob, plus a very gentle but malnourished and obviously ill Husky. She had a rasping cough that was accompanied by alarming sputum that suggested a terminal ailment. If you'd heard it in a human, you'd have called it a graveyard cough.

I retired to bed almost immediately, but upon going downstairs the next morning, Michael emphatically stated that this dog would not be staying with us. Clearly, Sharon and the kids delighted in her, but I was unable to share their pleasure. And sure enough, a mere two hours later I took a phone call from the owner's sister who had seen one of Sharon's notices.

It transpired that the dog, whose name was Belle, belonged to a guy who was building a barn just a few hundred metres up the road from where we lived. It wasn't clear why the sister was making the call, but she promised that her brother would ring us soon to arrange to collect his lost pet. The call came within a few minutes and a very non-plussed individual told me that he'd come and pick up his dog shortly. Four hours passed before the dogs alerted me to the fact that there was a vehicle at the front gate, which I'd left unlocked since his call. I hurried out just in time to see Belle being led away towards a truck. The guy shouted a cursory word of thanks over his shoulder, but watching through the gate, I will always be haunted by the backward glance that Belle cast me. I imagined I saw a strange mixture of regret and gratitude.

We never saw or heard of Belle again. Yet unbeknownst to us at that moment, in that brief time of sharing our home with us she had probably had a greater affect upon our lives than any dog since Kaiti. Even today the impact of that brief fostering has had repercussions beyond anybody's wildest imagination. As you will see, it requires quite a lot of explanation.

A uniquely special dog: Sage's tale

I won't pretend to have formed the bond with Belle that Sharon and the children did. She was in my life for less than sixteen hours and I was asleep for nine of them. I was certainly impressed by her quiet dignity and tolerance of what might have been a very strange environment, but my feelings didn't extend beyond that.

For Sharon, her departure left a very definite 'Husky hole'; but she had no desire to fill it. From my perspective Belle had been an aberration in our lives. I didn't even care for the breed so I was anxious to shut the door on this particular dog chapter. Whilst Sharon contacted the humane societies to let them know the good news of Belle's owner reunion, I went to delete the entry Sharon had made on the lost/found website.

I never found the website. I never deleted the entry. Instead, I was curiously sidetracked.

By a strange twist of fate that would be unexplainable to most, I found myself on the British Columbia Husky Rescue website, without even realising what I was looking at. Instead of lost dog ads I was faced with tragic tales of unwanted dogs. I managed to inure myself to them until I came to one that showed a stunning eight year old Husky whose name was Sage. I read her history without emotion then moved on. After a few minutes more I closed down the internet in frustration at my inability to find Sharon's ad and thought no more of it.

The next day I was working on the computer when, almost without realising it, found myself back on the BCHR site. I looked for the dog again and sat regarding her photo for a long while before leaving the site to do something more productive. But when I found myself doing the same thing again the next day, I called Sharon in to see the dog. She too found Sage to be very impressive so we admired her briefly together before affirming to each other that we most certainly didn't need another dog!

However, across the next three weeks I found myself visiting the site almost every day to see if Sage had been adopted yet. I quickly came to realise that the lot of an older dog in a rescue centre is not filled with hope and that she would likely be in there for a long time, if indeed she would ever be rescued.

If I missed viewing her for a couple of days Michael would suggest to me that I visit the site. I even made mention to Sharon that such a beautiful creature was still there but she refused to even listen and insisted that I make no further mention of it.

Then during the third week Michael asked if we would consider taking her. He explained that she wasn't an avatar, but that she would fit in with the pack and not be troublesome. My reply was very much "thanks, but no thanks". I knew that Sharon would find the suggestion intolerable and that I risked a heated confrontation if I pushed the issue.

The following weekend we went snowshoeing with Scott and Shannon north of Lake Louise and had arranged to spend the night at the Fairmont Chateau in celebration of Shannon's birthday. The following day, Sharon and I returned via Banff where we stopped to get a coffee and I was a little dismayed that Michael kept mentioning Sage. More out of exasperation than anything else, I asked for physical ratification of the veracity of his message and within seconds, I had seen a stuffed Husky toy and a book that featured huskies on the cover. Neither of these things is particularly out of the ordinary but my work requires that I be an unusually observant person and despite having visited Banff on many previous occasions, neither of these things had ever filtered into my consciousness before today.

Then in the distance I noticed a tail sticking out from behind an object that obstructed our view of its owner. Sharon noticed it at the same time and asked "What sort of dog is that?" "I don't know" I replied, adding very quietly "But if it's a Husky it's the third sign". My mumblings did not escape Sharon's attention but she made no comment. As we approached the distant creature, sure enough, a Husky came in to view, but still Sharon said nothing. We finished our visit and returned to the car; then as we were driving out of the town she said "What did you mean: the third sign? Is this about that dog on the rescue site?"

She was clearly very much less than pleased but Michael was loud and clear in my head telling me to reveal the whole story and this time I didn't disobey.

Frankly there wasn't much to tell because Sharon knew as much as I did about her background. But there was the addition that Michael had asked us to consider taking her and that fact alone drew Sharon's attention. "What will happen to the dog if we don't take her?" she asked: The reply the was instant and heartbreaking: "Her life will be very short lived."

I could hear the rising emotion catch in Sharon's throat and I found myself struggling to see the road through tears. There was a pause as we both composed ourselves and then she asked if he could tell us any more about the dog. What followed was totally beyond our experiences and understanding to date:

Although not an avatar, Sage was a special dog. By an accident of birth (that has never been explained to us) she had been born with an infusion of adamantine particles.

What are adamantine particles?

Adamantine particles are the elements from which everything is made. They are the building blocks of creation. They are present in everything from the foods we eat to the air we breathe. They compromise our bodies, the trees, the oceans, the earth itself.

These were very difficult for her body, which was that of a normal dog, to tolerate. It meant that energetically she was prone to respond to impulses within her physical frame that might sometimes make her appear odd; but more importantly it could make those around her feel uncomfortable. Thus throughout her life she had been rejected by those homes in which she found herself. She had lived in many households, pounds, rescues and on the streets. She was certainly not a bad dog (in fact a most gentle creature) but she could easily be misjudged as a result of the unsettling affects she created.

Adamantine particles in animals

There are occasions across our linear time history where animals that have been infused with adamantine particles are gifted to us. They are seldom recognised by those who are not more versed in the true nature of the world around us and they are only sent when they are needed. Principally this has been to indigenous peoples who are struggling to live their lives honouring the earth and its creatures and living in synergy with it.

The animal may take any form but such occurrences are most widely known in buffalo and elephants. They are most obviously recognised by the fact that they are white. They are not necessarily albinos or the freaks of nature that scientists would have us believe, but gifts to assist us in times of great need.

The creature that hosts such a concentration of adamantine, whilst apparently physically 'normal' has been specially prepared to withstand the demands that the particles create upon its structure. This means that whilst any individual may certainly be able to experience that the animal has a different energy, they do not create the discomfort that Sage did.

A dog infused in this manner would be virtually unknown and Sage should not have had the particles. Michael did explain that it was not a 'full load', just a limited amount; but still enough to make her capable of supporting manifestation.

Not all white animals possess adamantine particles by any means. It is *very* rare. So if you own a white animal, don't get too excited!

This was enough for Sharon and she gave her assent for a ninth dog, but Michael had more to say: Because she possessed the adamantine particles, the affect of this upon our household would be that if we were able to fully focus, they could be utilised to manifest that which was for our highest good.

What is manifestation?

Manifestation is the ability to create at will. It is most familiar to people as a result of the bestselling book 'The Secret' although in actual fact, it's no secret at all. We have always had the ability to manifest and create through thought in both a positive and negative way. However, the true extent to which we are able to do this is seldom reached because of the degree of focus that is required.

For us this sounded a bit like having a magic wishing dog that would grant our every desire! Upon hearing this you would think we would experience wild happiness and start planning to have our every need fulfilled, but we were only too aware of the consequences of misusing this gift. Rather than rush to focus our attentions on what we could create if we got the dog, we turned our attentions to the more practical issues of making sure that we were able to become her new guardians.

Adamantine particles and manifestation

Native American peoples are well familiar with the significance of a white buffalo being born. It heralds a time a great joy, peace and prosperity and so it is regarded as sacred.

However, the reason for the effect that the animal seems to create is due to its infusion of adamantine particles. Those people who are in its proximity are close to an unusually massive concentration of the building blocks of creation and thus, through thought alone they can bring about what they desire.

Of course, this can be abused and varying desires may counter one another. But historically, when the focus of a whole tribe has been upon surviving, which develops into security and then comfort and then prosperity as expectations are raised, it can be seen why these stages in the progression of tribal life could easily be achieved across the lifetime of such a beast.

Their birth is rare and now ever increasingly so. This is because the needs of our cultures are notionally more sophisticated and individually conflicting. If they are seen nowadays, these sacred animals are there more as a sign.

When we got home I contacted the rescue in British Columbia where Sage was being sheltered and after going through the vetting procedures and an extended dialogue with the lady who was currently fostering Sage, arrangements were made for her to be shipped to us a few weeks before Christmas.

I had already researched the breed thoroughly and we made preparations to receive a strong willed and somewhat aloof dog that would most likely prefer to live outside. We knew that she would require 'experienced' handling just to gain her respect and that without this she would potentially decide to be dominant over all of us.

Two weeks later when we arrived at the cargo handling depot the flight from Comox had already arrived and there was only a brief delay before we were able to go and collect the crate with Sage inside. We were shown into the warehouse area where a solitary crate was surrounded by workers staring silently at an unmoving creature inside. Seeing us coming towards them they quickly dispersed but one remained to tell us that it was a "fine looking dog we had there". We took our first look at Sage and I almost gasped. The pictures had not done her justice as there sat a stunning, almost radiant, silver and white Husky with a long lustrous coat. The only thing amiss was that she would not look at anyone. She made no response to anyone who tried to get her attention and her gaze was firmly fixed on the back of the crate.

We wasted no time in letting her out of the crate and into the back of the car before beginning yet another journey back from the airport with a dog on board. As we travelled, we tried to engage Sage, but her misery was obvious and all pervasive. We tried to be cheery and draw her out, but to no avail. We lapsed into discussing the strangeness of being the owners of a Husky since it was not a breed in which we had even the remotest interest prior to Belle's appearance. As a youth in the UK my brother had a friend whose family were Canadian and had brought two huskies across with them. I had never seen them and only had reports of their good nature. To me they seemed to be mysterious, even exotic

150

dogs; but I never aspired to own one. And now here we were with an amazing example of the breed, albeit a very depressed and sad one.

When we got home it was dark and we parked the car just inside the gate, ensured that it was properly closed and then opened the hatchback. Sage stood up and for the first time we could really appreciate just how awesome she was. As she jumped out of the car, a transformation seemed to overtake her being. It was as if her confidence and interest in life was being restored and she bounded off to explore the grounds. We took the unusual step of letting all of the dogs out to meet her in one go and far from being intimidated, she seemed to accept their attentions easily and with good grace. There was no hostility from either side and after a matter of minutes the others seemed to have accepted her as one of the pack. Perhaps the particles within her created a certain aura. Perhaps she simply had the confidence necessary to have survived a tough life and living off her wits. Whatever, she fit right in.

Over the next few days Sage quickly established herself as a house Husky. There was to be none of this living outside nonsense! It's an easy thing for any pet owner to anthropomorphise, but I was convinced that she was grateful, although it wasn't always obvious. I believe it was an aspect of her past experience that made her slightly wary of us and unwilling to receive any kind of affection when the other dogs were present. She was every bit as forthcoming as the others when it came to feeding time, but otherwise, she made sure that she kept her distance. She seemed to find it difficult to accept that she had a place that was her own in the house and despite having put out a brand new bed for her, at night we could hear her pacing the rooms below and in the mornings she was most often to be found on the carpet behind a sofa. However, as the days passed she began to warm up a little and I remember feeling that we had come to a real turning point when we were returning from shopping one day and she not only rushed to meet the car as it came towards the fence, she also demanded attention just as the others always did. That night as I was putting everybody to bed, I found Sage curled up on her own bed and as I knelt beside her, she did not flinch or shirk away from the physical contact I offered. She let me rest my head on her astounding coat and was, perhaps for the first time,

151

totally relaxed. It was then that I noticed an amazing energy that seemed to emanate from her body, but I dismissed it as fantasy.

At breakfast the next morning, Sage came and stood beside me, hoping to get a piece of my toast. I remembered the energy field and moved my hand towards her. I was shocked to discover that when it was around 12 inches away that I could feel a very palpable pulsing that made my hand tingle all over. Excitedly, I called Sharon over and sure enough, without being told what to expect, she too was aghast to experience the same sensation. Later on that morning our friend Beth was coming to visit in her capacity as an insurance agent. We did not know if she shared our beliefs in spiritual matters since we had never discussed them with her so it was with some confidence in her neutrality that we asked her to indulge us and hold her hand over Sage's back. When she got about 8 inches away from the fur she let out a loud and shocked gasp of "Woah!" and quickly pulled her hand away. "Oh my God! What is that? My hand has suddenly got pins and needles." So we weren't just a couple of crazies letting our imaginations run away with us. Even 'normal' people could tell that there was something special about this dog.

This seemed to be confirmed when on Christmas Eve we made the second of what has become our annual pilgrimage to Lake Louise. That year we took Dougal, Indy and Sage. Usually Indy is a show stopper. People are awed at his size and magnificence. They have rarely seen a member of the breed. Dougal has always been a crowd pleaser and his presence has opened more conversations than any of our dogs. But this time it was very different. By the time we had walked 400 metres I had received three requests to photograph Sage and before we left, I counted seventeen people that asked about her or wanted to photograph her. That day it was as if Indy was invisible and poor old Dougal didn't get a look in!

I had it in mind that Sage would make a great ski-jor dog (a dog that pulls you whilst you are on skis) as she seemed to pull quite well, so to see how she was, I ran the whole length of Lake Louise with her at roughly the same pace as if she were towing me on skis. She seemed to love it. As we waited at the far end for the others, she sat patiently until they arrived and we posed for a family photo. It was a particularly good one and still one of our favourites. We sent it to friends and relatives all over the world, proudly pointing out our new family member and I was especially pleased to send one to the lovely lady who had been fostering Sage. She sent a touching reply, telling us how she wished she could have been there with us and how pleased she was that Sage had found such happiness at last.

Oddly, up until this point Sharon had found it a little more difficult to warm to Sage than I had. Belle had immediately been a warm and accepting dog with obvious affection for her. She had hoped that Sage would be the same but despite going out of her way to make her feel welcome and at home, the dog did not seem to respond to her positively and was quite stand-offish towards her. But later that evening I found Sharon with her head buried in Sage's fur as they enjoyed a quiet moment together On the night before Christmas, Sage decided that our bedroom, already shared by four of the others, was to be hers also. She took up a vacant position on the floor at the foot of the bed and we were delighted that finally, she had accepted both of us and our home as hers.

If you have slept in a room with dogs you probably know that they snore, break wind and dream just like humans do! Their dreams are often accompanied by odd yelps and even barks, so I was not really surprised when I was woken four nights later by a sound from Sage that was exactly like a scream. It was strange but huskies are renowned for their odd noises and they really do try to talk rather than bark. I got out of bed and gently shook her leg until she stopped dreaming, my tried and test technique for doing so. I went back to sleep and we all passed the rest of the night peacefully.

The next morning I got up and went to the en suite, blearily passing a still sleeping Sage and wading through the others who were up and about and eagerly awaiting their breakfasts. When I came out again, Sharon remarked that Sage, normally enthusiastic for food herself by this time, was having a lie in. I looked down at her and held my breath before I replied: "She's dead."

Dogs reincarnate

Sharon and I knelt by Sage's lifeless form, burying our fingers in her gorgeous coat. We had shared her life for just three weeks and six days and it was incomprehensible that she was gone already. But her body was long dead and an almost surreal grief slowly began to conquer over our sense that she would wake up at any moment. I was numbed. Sharon sat shaking her head saying over and over again: "This isn't right. This isn't right". It was a full five minutes before we were able to uproot ourselves and overcome the paralysis of the shock we felt. We broke the news to the kids and a general wailing was to be heard all around the house. In the midst of this unhappiness I observed that the other dogs were seemingly indifferent. None of them went to inspect the body. None of them showed any interest whatsoever. At first I took this as callousness before Michael put me right.

Why were the dogs indifferent?

Whilst animals may certainly grieve for a lifelong friend who has moved on, Sage had not been part of the pack long enough for the others to have developed a close bond with her and thus they were unlikely to miss her.

However, animals are innately more knowledgeable about the 'true' ways of the world than we are. They have a better understanding of the nature of their existence and the meaninglessness of concepts such as life and death. They know that the essence of another creature will return if it is appropriate for it to do so and therefore their emotional response to death can be quite matter-of-fact.

We tried to get on with the everyday chores of living since it was obviously business as usual for the other dogs. An hour later the whole family was gathered on the sofas in front of the fireplace and a tearful Sharon was still angrily asserting that a great injustice had transpired. "Michael said that her life would be short lived if she *didn't* come to us and we took her, so why is she dead now?" she sobbed, unable to keep a slight bitterness from her tone.

Channelling when you are upset yourself is not that easy but it was clear that explanations were needed, so I tuned in.

Michael came through gently but firmly: "You did not ask what would come to pass if she came to live with you." The irony of our assumptions hit home with full force. We had viewed ourselves as the rescuers who had saved her from certain death and it was a struggle to place ourselves in the role we were now experiencing. He went on: "There *is* reason and purpose in what has taken place and if you wish to understand I will explain it to you. But if you choose to blame or feel guilt you will be unable to grasp the full import of what I will reveal."

We were silenced and he went on to explain very fully that Sage had indeed been grateful for us having taken her into our home. But her life prior to arrival with us had altered her state of being. She had no chance of achieving the balance that would have enabled her progress along her ascension pathway. She had not lived a synergistic life with humans and she still experienced difficulty in both giving and receiving love. Her higher self had seen the futility of the situation and had let her die.

Then Michael asked a heart stopping question: "Would you like her back?"

I gasped as I began to understand the full implications of what he was saying: Animals reincarnate just like humans. Not only do they come back but he was about to tell me how we could find her again. A very red eyed family sat looking at each other in awe as all agreed "Yes, we would like her back" and the explanation continued:

Sage's higher self had decided to take a calculated risk. It had quickly recognised that due to the somewhat unique energies within our household, had she been raised by us from birth, she could not only have achieved balance but also ascended. It had decided to gamble that if she were to die we would be prepared to take her back. Up until the point where Sharon had finally bonded with her, it had not been confident that we would say yes. But at the point where Sage had felt

156

totally accepted, the higher self had decided that the risk was worth taking. It had withdrawn the protection that it was able to give Sage's physical body that prevented the adamantine particles from having a destructive affect upon her. Without this, the power of the energetic flow they possessed became too much for her physical form. As a consequence, she had suffered a massive stroke and died. Now she was free to return and fulfil her potential, but only if we could track her down and get her back. All by itself, this process was fraught with even greater risks for Sage's soul.

How had Sage's higher self been able to intervene?

Although a human being's free will is sacrosanct and ability of the higher self to impact upon our lives is relatively limited, this is not the case with animals. Their higher selves may intervene directly in their lives in situations that involve life and death. For the purposes of their ascension pathway and the learning which they may glean from a lifetime, there are fewer opportunities available to them whilst they are the pets of humans than there are for the humans themselves. As a consequence, when presented with an opportunity to withdraw and start again, the higher self will use its discretion to decide the earthbound fate of its physical incarnation.

Basically it can ask the question: Is there benefit in staying and is there more learning that can be achieved in these circumstances?

Interestingly, it looks from the perspective of the human as well as the animal. Even though the animal itself may derive no benefit, if the human can, then the animal will always stay until it is physically unable to do so.

This does not mean that the higher self can randomly kill off its earthly manifestation! Occasions for making such choices only arise in very particular circumstances. These would include: when the animal has been involved in an accident; when the animal has a life threatening illness; when the animal is being operated on; or, as in Sage's case, where the animal's whole life is lived on a perpetual knife edge. It makes

157

the choice always with a focus upon the ascension of the creature and it is always acting in its best interests.

Still in shock I went and sat in front of the computer whilst Michael gave precise details of where and when she would be due to come back. Sure enough, a breeder in Ontario that he directed me to would be having a litter in six months time and this would be where Sage would return.

It was now crucial that I be able to get the pick of the litter. Although Michael would certainly tell me which of the newborn puppies was Sage, if I could not choose the right one because I did not have the first pick, she could be lost to us forever. Within the hour I had made contact with the breeder and was at the top of the waiting list for the puppies. Everything seemed fine and for the first time that morning, the tidal wave of sadness that had threatened to engulf us all started to recede.

However, we were still left with the sad task of disposing of Sage's body. This required us to take her to the vet who duly confirmed that she had died of a heart attack following a massive stroke. As we came to leave, the receptionist who was also the vet's wife raised the question that I had known was coming but greeted with dread: "Would you like her body to be cremated?" I had heard nightmarish stories of animals being cremated in bulk incinerators where the returned ashes bore no connection to the pet the owners had cherished in life. It was a cynical money making scheme to cash in on the grief of vulnerable people and I wanted no part of it.

Even though I knew that in the big scheme of things, it was of no consequence at all, in that moment it seemed the most important question on earth. "How do we know it's her ashes we'll get back?" I managed to whisper the words before I could no longer hold it together. I broke down in shuddering sobs that left me breathless. Only Sharon's light touch on my arm kept me from going into paroxysms of grief. It must have been a pathetic sight to see a grown man so distraught and out of control, but the vet wife's was more than sympathetic. With a very gentle manner she reassured me that she knew the man who carried out the cremations personally. He always treated deceased animals with the utmost respect and they had sent their own pets to him in the past. Sage would be well looked after and it would most definitely be her ashes that were returned to us. I nodded my agreement and left, leaving Sharon who was a lot stronger than me at this point, to deal with the details.

As we left, even in spite of everything that I now knew, I felt that we were leaving Sage behind and it was only when a beautiful handmade box adorned with a brass plaque containing her ashes was returned to us was few days later that things felt 'right' again. We also took great comfort from the 'In Sympathy' card we received from the vet and his wife. It may seem like a ridiculous thing to send for those who do not love animals as we do; from our perspective it was a highly sensitive gesture demonstrating true empathy that we valued enormously.

Sage was the first of our dogs that we had lost. She had only been with us for twenty seven days yet the impact that she had upon us was astonishing. Consideration of all of these issues left me slightly uneasy concerning how strong my reaction would be if one of the others who had been with us for longer departed. I mulled over the knowledge that the avatars could never return and felt this knowledge as tangible pain. Yet in the midst of all of this, we all recognised how lucky we were to know that at least Sage was already on her way back to us.

More than an afterthought: Lara's tale

I now need to go back in the story to the point where Michael directed me to Sage's next point of incarnation:

After I had found the site Michael directed me to and found the breeders where Sage would be returning, I sat and trawled the net further, seemingly without purpose. I came upon another Husky breeder's site in Saskatchewan. It showed attractive pictures of their dogs and I viewed it with detached interest until Michael delivered the knowledge that they had one puppy from a recent litter available. Furthermore, if we were to buy it, even though it was already a week old, its body would be taken by an avatar that would enter as a 'walk-in'.

What is a 'walk-in'?

The term walk-in is used to describe the entry of an angelic soul into a place where another soul is already present.

For the briefest of time they may co-exist while the consciousness of the one suppresses that of the other. When there is a wholesale removal of the soul in favour of the incoming soul, it then becomes an avatar.

I called to Sharon who, although pleased over the fact that we had notionally managed to secure Sage's return, was still dealing with the upset over her. I explained what Michael had just said, and perhaps because of the on-going grief, she was a little more receptive to the suggestion of yet another dog than she might otherwise have been. However, she still wanted to know what the purpose of this dog would be? Michael explained that the suggestion would never have been made had we not agreed to let Sage return to us. The avatar wished to experience a relationship with the returning dog. This would not only assist in the avatar's desired experience, it would also make Sage's progress on the ascension pathway easier.

We debated it for a few minutes and considered the merits of having two huskies. They are pack animals so from their perspective, having another of their own breed of nearly the same age would be a blast. If we had two, I could definitely take up ski-jor. Since Michael had already said that the available puppy was a bitch, they would be like sisters and perhaps that was the experience that the avatar wanted? And it would make us a five avatar household! One way or another, it wasn't such a bad idea, so we agreed.

I contacted the breeder and he confirmed that there was one female available. Since they had only just been born, we would have seven weeks to wait before we could collect her so we would remain in contact and set things up nearer the time. Within minutes of the phone call and the agreement being reached, Michael confirmed that the avatar had walked into the body. I felt again the curious mixture of amusement and guilt that came from knowing that another breeder had an angel in their midst without ever knowing it. Although the breeder had already given her the kennel name Haley, after much debate we decided that we would call her Lara.

The weeks passed quickly and it was soon time for me to make the journey to collect the puppy from Saskatchewan, a round trip of around nineteen hours. I was trying to work out where it would be best to stay when the breeder rang to ask if I would consider a proposal that might make life easier for both of us. He was shipping a sister dog called Lily to the US and the only direct flight to the destination left from our local airport. If I would agree to take the sister to the airport and deliver her to the cargo handlers, he would meet me at a town on the border between Saskatchewan and Alberta, a mere seven hour round trip. This would save me gas money and the cost of an overnight stay. I guesstimated that I would be at least $240 better off. All I had to do was accept the responsibility for getting her on the flight. However, since Lily had to be with the cargo people by 11.30am on the day that I collected her, we agreed to meet at 7.30am. this would give us time to complete the various bits of paperwork and still allow me plenty of time to get back to the airport which was two and half hours away.

I got up at 3.00m on the day of Lara's collection and was on the road by 3.30am. I'm one of those people who would rather be an hour early than a minute late and let somebody down, so leaving a half hour window for any delays seemed like a sound thing to do. The journey went without major incident and I arrived at our designated collection point at 7.00am exactly.

Despite his commitment on timings the breeder arrived an hour and a half later, by which time I was decidedly edgy. Already I was facing a journey to the airport that only left me a half hour margin for delay, and we still had the paperwork to go over. He made no apology for his late arrival and when I was finally able to get away with my two new charges, I had no delay margin left. I had also received the horrifying news that the puppies had been fed just an hour before he had arrived.

I pulled away in my vehicle, feeling the pressure of the knowledge that I had to be at the airport on time. But I only managed to get two kilometres before it was spectacularly confirmed that the puppies had recently eaten. I pulled into a gas station and it took ten minutes to clear up the mess. Unlike my experience in Germany where I had not been equipped to deal with Indy's stress relief, at least this time I had paper towels and antiseptic spray. It was Lara's sister who had performed so I put both of them into Lara's clean crate whilst I cleaned the other. When all was done, I transferred her back and set out again. I got another half a kilometre before Lara performed and the whole process started all over again. Twenty five kilometres later, they both performed and I had a deficit in the time available to get to the airport.

Fortunately for me, the roads on the route to the airport were straight and empty and the landscape was very open. It was possible to go very fast without the risk of encountering any unexpected police vehicles and my satellite navigation slowly began to demonstrate that I was gaining back enough lost time to arrive at the airport without missing the deadline. Nonetheless, I felt the need to gain a little time, despite Michael's assurances that I would arrive without any problems. The angelic realms would 'stretch' time for me, so I should not be so flustered.

What did Michael mean about stretching time?

It was very soon after I had begun channelling that Michael explained the concept of stretching time to me.

163

Our concept of time being a linear progression is an unrealistic concept that we need in order to try to get an understanding of where we are relative to anything else.

In actual fact he said, time loops and is best expressed as a diagram with many intersections and overlaps that looks a bit like a Spirograph picture created with one of those toys from the late 1960s.

The speed at which time passes is an illusion that we create for ourselves. Consequently, we can make it go faster or slower. Mostly we speed it up and find ourselves in the position where vast amounts of time have passed us by without even realising it.

As they grow older adults often report the experience that time seems to go by faster and faster. It doesn't because time is an illusion, but their perception creates that reality for them.

Confused? Me too!

So Michael explained that if I ever needed more time all I had to do was ask for it and that 'extensions' would be created that effectively stretched time.

Over the years, I've had many causes to use it, mostly to avoid being late for events. The most spectacular of these was when I had an appointment in London which began with a fifty minute train journey, a ten minute ride on the London Underground followed by a ten minute walk. Add to this the time taken to get from the train to the underground and assuming that an underground train was there the second I arrived on the platform, I was looking at the need for at least an eighty minute window if I was to reach my destination on time.

Being me, I left myself two hours but that morning the train was delayed. I paced the platform for over an hour, becoming progressively more stressed and when the journey finally began, I had only fifty minutes in total before the meeting was due to start. Arriving on time would clearly be a physical impossibility so I telephoned ahead and warned them that I would be quite late.

> Upon boarding the train I sat down, closed my eyes and requested a time extension. Not once did I look at my watch after that.
>
> Both the client and I had cause to be surprised upon my eventual arrival since, despite my telephoned warning, I arrived exactly on time.
>
> Bizarre as it may sound, I would testify to the truth of this story on my most solemn oath.

I ignored Michael's promise to my cost.

About one hour away from the airport I arrived at a section of the road where there were bends and trees blocking my vision. As I raced around one of them, I found myself staring at a police patrol vehicle coming the other way and the blare of his siren seemed to instantaneously fill my ears. I pulled over and the officer got out to perform his duties. I felt sick to the pit of my stomach but he was a nice guy and he was polite enough not to comment on the ghastly stench that was coming from the back of the car. I tried to rationalise my driving by explaining the pressure I was under, but it cut no muster. The law was the law and I had been doing 138km in a 100km zone. The fine would cost me $260.

By the time we were done, I looked at the clock and saw that I would miss the deadline at the cargo handlers. I was shaken by the experience of getting a ticket as I prefer to abide by the speed limits; and so for the rest of the journey I drove with the cruise control fixed to the limit. I wasn't going to do any more rushing around today. I began to try to figure out how I could get round the expense of having to get the puppy on another flight when Michael again chipped in: "Don't worry; you will get there on time. Relax and do not allow yourself to become unbalanced by this experience."

Time wise it was impossible. By now I had forty minutes left and I was still an hour away from the airport. But you learn to trust angels when they make commitments to you so I stopped stressing, stopped thinking about having to pay and just went with the flow! And sure enough, I arrived at the cargo handlers with three minutes to spare. It absolutely should not have happened, but it did.

I bade farewell to Lily and I carried on my journey with only Lara.

Up until that point the puppies had provided company for one another. I had placed their crates so that they faced one another and they made only a few resentful sounds at having left all that was familiar to them. Now, faced with the desolation of no company, Lara began to demonstrate to me that she was truly a Husky. The amount of noise that came from her was remarkable. In strict sequence she howled; she sang; she did an incredible peacock impersonation; then to finish off her repertoire she demonstrated an uncanny ability to say the word "burr" long and loud as if the word were being uttered by a human. And then she would start all over again.

It was with an immense sigh of relief that I arrived home, almost deafened. After being welcomed by Sharon, we orchestrated her meetings with the other dogs by letting them out one by one, with me standing by to ensure that all went well. It did, with no problems whatsoever and Lara was accepted as part of the pack.

Can I get Melody back?

In the week after Sage's death and before we got Lara, I had the painful task of letting both the fosterer and British Columbia Husky Rescue know what had come to pass. The fosterer had Sage for six months before she came to us so naturally, she was beside herself and grieved every bit as much as we did and probably more. After all, she had known her for longer.

Although I knew that I shouldn't, I felt incredibly guilty that an animal that had been lovingly entrusted to us had died. It was as if somehow we had been responsible for what had happened. But the lady who ran the Husky rescue, Joanne, was terribly understanding, sympathetic and supportive. We began a correspondence as a result of a touching email that she sent to us regarding the Rainbow Bridge.

What is the Rainbow Bridge?

The concept of the Rainbow Bridge is a touching notion that is known to many animal lovers. It embodies the simple idea that a deceased animal, in transitioning from life to afterlife, has moved on over the Bridge to a happier place where it awaits the arrival of its beloved master(s).

If you look at the websites of many dog breeders or personal sites of animal lovers, you often see lovingly written obituaries and poems that help both the authors and readers deal with their grief. Personally, they never fail to move me to the point where I am no longer able to read them.

It is a fact seldom accepted by those who are not animal lovers that the grief experienced upon the death of a pet can be even worse than that experienced upon the death of a human. To us they are every bit as important in our relationships as many human beings.

We pet owners feel bereft because we are unable to communicate as fully with our animals as we would wish. Although we trust that our pets know of our great love for them, we wish we could have expressed it more amply. We want them to know how important they are to us and how much we will miss and grieve for them. Seemingly, we are denied a common language with which to express these words; we can never be sure that they understand and thus the pain of parting is all the more intense.

The idea that they are waiting for us over the Rainbow Bridge is therefore an enormously comforting one because it allows us hope that we will see our animals again and have the opportunity to demonstrate our joy in the reunion.

However, the reality of animal reincarnation is that it is much the same as our own. After passing over, they have the opportunity to review their past life and plan for the next.

Perhaps this is even more comforting than the idea that having crossed over the Rainbow Bridge, it is all over for them, as it most certainly is not!

After a few days, I felt guided to share our knowledge that Sage was coming back with Joanne.

When you open up something like this to anyone, there is always the risk that your beliefs are ridiculed. But I didn't want this particular lady to develop any doubts about us, so it was with some trepidation that I pushed the 'send' button with my email announcing this news. To my great relief, its content sparked considerable interest and we began a lengthy series of emails wherein I explained to her all of the factors associated with Sage's untimely death.

Since it concerned issues that I didn't fully understand myself at that time, it was enormously helpful that she asked many questions that Michael provided answers for. In that respect we both grew. We got to know one another quite well and it transpired that as well as running Husky rescue, she was a greatly respected breeder, highly knowledgable about the breed.

Then came the day when she told me about her still raw feelings of grief over the loss of one her dogs some time before. She had owned a breathtaking animal called Melody who was not only a champion show dog, but had also been a movie star and a wonderful companion to her. She amongst all the dogs Joanne had owned and still owned, had been the stand-out. She sent me a photograph (which I still have on my wall) that positively radiated the goodness from within the animal. The loss of such a treasured companion haunted this caring lady and she wanted to know if I could find out where and when she was coming back?

Excitedly I tuned in and asked Michael, delighted that I could be of service to such a kind being. But the answer would prove to be massively disappointing for both of us: Melody would not return. She had no need to. She had achieved balance and fulfilled her learning on the earthly planes and had chosen to go on. She was confident that Joanne would be fine without her. They had already learnt from one another all that was necessary. Whilst Melody empathised with Joanne's grief, she knew that one of life's biggest lessons was about letting go and to this end, it was time for her to move on. This act in itself would provide the greater opportunity for growth. She was effectively being cruel to be kind.

<u>Why wouldn't Melody come back?</u>

Having gone through all of the necessary learning experiences and having achieved balance, there was simply no need for Melody to come back.

However, she would have had the choice. She could come back to assist another on their ascension pathway and if this were the case, she would be encumbered by her own development needs.

In all likelihood, two pressing factors came into play in her decision: at the time at which Joanne asked me the question, it was already over a year after her death and therefore at least six months past the time when she would have been eligible for reincarnation. She had already made the decision not to return and so would have been preparing for her next life in another form.

Parts of that decision not to return would most certainly have been based on the uncertainties that animal reincarnation presents for the creature. She would have been aware that there was no-one to guide Joanne to her, so she could have elected to reincarnate in a litter that was proximate to Joanne. Since Joanne was a breeder, that presented possibilities to her, but if no litters were planned, she would have to risk coming back somewhere where it was 'supposed to happen' that Joanne would get a puppy.

However, as already stated, there is always the risk of the intervention of free will. Joanne might not have got a puppy she had otherwise been 'meant' to. Somebody else might have got to Melody before she did. New and unplanned events could have occurred in Joanne's life. There are a myriad horde of reasons why they might not have been able to reconnect and this alone could have caused Melody to decline to return.

However, the overriding reason related to Joanne's needs and the act of not returning was ultimately a totally unselfish one. Despite how she felt, Joanne did not need Melody. In accepting her departure and progress she could learn more than she ever could from her return.

It was very sad, but appropriate.

I know that Joanne was upset by the answer because I was to. She was brave about it because she was pleased that the creature she doted on had been successful in its spiritual journey; but her heart still longed to be with Melody again.

I was able to provide only limited consolation on this score as a result of what Michael had explained; but I would have loved to have helped her more and it gave me cause for considerable reflection upon our beloved pets. I wondered if Michael would present me with more opportunities to help others be reunited with their lost animals.

Coming out

Even if I wanted to help others on one level, on another I was still a reluctant purveyor of messages. I worried about what it would do to my credibility, my career and my life in general. Even to me, all of the things that were being revealed to me seemed to stretch the boundaries of belief to an almost impossible level. I couldn't conceive of having to tell (those who were completely uninitiated in any aspect of this 'weirdness') things related to unseen beings who either had wings or seemed to have lived lifetimes centuries ago.

From the earliest time that I was learning to channel, my four guides had made it quite clear to me that this was not a 'gift' that I possessed without reason. It was always intended that I use it for the highest good of all. I was OK with this within the limited scope of my existing personal channelling sessions with like-minded individuals, but beyond that I was fearful.

Even in this arena I already had uncomfortable experiences with those who knew that I channelled: some supposed that I talked to dead people (mediumship); others that I knew things about them in advance or heard private details of their every intimacy. I have an uncomfortable recollection of spending some time with a lady who was constantly on edge and struggling to deal with my presence in her house, despite having invited me there. She would start a sentence, pause midway through and give me a funny look. "But I guess you already know that..." she would trail off. She was disappointed when it became apparent that I didn't know anything and I had to explain that I am only privy to information that is for the highest good of the individual and the highest good of all. Things are not revealed to me without there being a very specific reason for my needing to know them.

Other individuals seemed to think that the angels would spontaneously open dialogue with them through me at every available opportunity. I got used to hearing the question: "So do they have anything to say to me right now?" and watching the disappointment when I say "No". Sharon and I were once at a restaurant for a friend's birthday party. Eventually the time came when we had to leave to get back for the

171

dogs. Apparently after we had gone one of the other guests expressed her disappointment. She had been waiting all evening for me to come and talk to her since she was convinced that Archangel Michael would wish to send her a message!

On the other hand I had remarkable experiences of being asked to give information to people that was never rejected, even when it was unusual and out-of-context, such as that which I received whilst running a class for a business client:

It was the third week of a three week program that had been spread across a year. Between the first and second events one of the participants had become pregnant, and now she was only 6 weeks away from giving birth. Her presence on what was a very physical program was of her own volition and she coped admirably. Whilst I was presenting to the group on the first morning I was scanning the room and my eyes fell upon Rachel. Her physical state was inescapable but I paid little attention until Michael interrupted me. "That's a Rainbow child she's carrying" he said inside my head. I continued my presentation without missing a beat but he continued: "You need to tell her". I hesitated for a fraction of a second whilst I confirmed what he'd just said. Having simultaneous conversations like this is something I'm quite used to so it's not too difficult (unless it gets very distracting) so I was able to reply without breaking off my presentation: "Maybe, but not right now!"

The next day Michael reminded me again of the need to tell Rachel. This time it was while she was leading a four hour exercise and I used the excuse that I couldn't distract her. Besides, I hadn't really got to know her that well. She was one of those participants who prefer to keep their distance and of the entire group, she was the only one who had never sat near me at lunch or dinner. How could I possibly go and tell a complete stranger, in a business setting, that I had a message from an Archangel about her unborn child?

Michael does not take no for an answer easily if it is an important issue, so regularly during the course of the week he would chip in with reminders. Each one I ignored and so by my closing presentation at the end of the week, the information had still not been passed on. Finally in frustration at being interrupted I agreed to tell her on condition that Michael create the circumstances.

Instantly I was left in peace. The program was brought to a close and we went in for dinner. I sat down first as usual so as to allow the opportunity for those who really wanted to chat to sit either beside me or opposite me and for those who'd had enough of me to escape further down the table. Much to my surprise and for the first time across all of our meals together, I found myself face-to-face with Rachel.

I then tried to surreptitiously reveal the information to Rachel without alerting the attentions of our fellow diners and without making it look like we were arranging some kind of secret tryst. I approached the matter in a very roundabout way and was pleasantly surprised that when I got to the final revelations, she was actually very interested. Over the course of the next hour and a half, I explained everything and she went away quite pleased with this new knowledge.

A few weeks later I received an email from Rachel. She had gone home and related to her partner everything that I had said. He had been captivated by the explanation and had revealed a spiritual side to himself and a series of beliefs that he had kept hidden from her for twelve years for fear of rejection. The information had revolutionised their lives.

With evidence like this to support my confidence, I began to feel a little less fearful, although Sharon had still dubbed me 'the reluctant channel'.

During one of Sharon's healing sessions a client had visited accompanied by a friend of hers called Wanda. As usual, I hid away in the basement office managing the nine dogs and trying to keep them from disrupting the tranquility of the moment as Sharon provided her ministrations. Via a convoluted route they had heard about me, and somewhat embarrassed, I was brought up to meet them.

It was to be a fateful encounter because from that point onward, Wanda became convinced that I should be channelling publicly in open forum and run classes for people locally concerning the vast amounts of knowledge that were being given to us about all and sundry. Once she had this idea, she wouldn't leave it alone. We were regularly contacted and moderate pressure was applied to encourage me to commence what she believed was my calling. I wasn't so sure.

Finally, after several months of this going on, I had a gentle nudge from Michael who affirmed that it was indeed one of my soul contracts that I should be doing more, and whilst I had freedom of choice about whether or not I wanted to do this, I had made a decision about what I *should* do before I ever incarnated.

What could I say?

Sharon and I went round to see Wanda and we agreed that I would deliver a quasi-public channelling session at her house followed by a question and answer session. The event went on for four hours and was to become the first of an on-going series of monthly sessions that I still deliver to this day. From the second one onwards, they were delivered in a local unity church and it was not long after that I began to deliver classes on achieving balance containing information that was entirely channelled.

The impact of revealing the information was not all good. As part of the process we set up a website to advertise what we were doing. It received a large number of hits, which unfortunately included some from business associates who had been researching me for work projects. When they saw what I was now doing, they seemed to assume that I had experienced some kind of mental breakdown, and in one case I lost a great deal of potential work.

So in spite of the fact that I was doing what I was supposed to be doing, the idea of approaching anybody on an uninvited basis with information that I was given was still a bit of an anathema to me. It was not so much an issue of the message itself, but inevitably there had to be a revelation of the source of the data. Although a nationwide survey in Canada revealed that 67% of the population believe in angels, I wasn't sure that they all wanted to hear from them!

174

Finding Buddy

My commitment to fulfilling my contract was tested yet again when Jenny came home from school one day and related to us some events that had come to pass. The main feature was the fact that one of the teacher's, Susan Palliser, had to leave school because she was so upset. Apparently one of her dogs, Buddy, had died the night before. She was a single lady and her dogs were like her children. Now she was beside herself with grief.

On the brief occasions when we had met Susan we had liked her immensely and this news was very saddening. We could relate to the experience that she must be going through and were discussing how she must be feeling when Michael intervened: "Tell her that you can get her dog back."

I stopped what I had been saying in mid sentence and Sharon and Jenny looked at me. I explained what I was being told and there followed a lengthy discussion on the practicalities of telling someone (who we had only come to know through parent teacher meetings) that their dog would reincarnate and that we could find it for them. We concluded that she would probably think we were crazy and despite my strong desire to help, we decided to do nothing about it.

Several weeks passed without any action on my part. Sharon went in to Jenny's school for parent teacher meetings. She met with Susan and expressed her sympathy for what Susan was going through but said nothing about Michael's suggestion.

More weeks passed and our neighbour Shannon came round for dinner one night. She taught at the same school as Susan and relayed the story of how Susan was still grieving over her lost pet. Furthermore, her other dog Wexford was very sick and in all likelihood, probably dying. Shannon was concerned with how Susan would react if she lost both of these treasured pets in such a short space of time, and so were we.

"Tell her that you can get her dog back." said Michael once more.

175

This time the potential opportunity for revealing this information to Susan seemed a bit clearer to me. I suggested that Shannon tell her that Sharon could help with Wexford. In the course of her energy healing work, Sharon has often helped out with dogs and previously had considerable success with Shannon's Bernese Mountain dogs. This had made Shannon something of a fan and recommending to Susan that Sharon could help would be something that Shannon would willingly do. For her part I knew that Sharon would love to help out with Wexford if she could. If we got through the door on this pretext, I could look for opportunities to mention Buddy.

As it turned out, Shannon not only told Susan about Sharon's healing abilities, she also mentioned, somewhat cryptically, that we could help her with Buddy!

That night we received a phone call from Susan who was desperate to know what Shannon had meant. Michael recommended that I not discuss it on the phone so I did my best to maintain her interest whilst being generally evasive. Susan is not a lady to let go easily and the experience was a little bit like being worried by a terrier. Eventually I managed to put her off with the promise that we would come round that coming weekend, Sharon would work on healing Wexford and I would explain what Shannon had meant regarding Buddy.

When we arrived at Susan's house that weekend we were welcomed into a room filled with pictures of Buddy and Wexford. Their importance to Susan was readily apparent. They had both been some kind of Shi-Tzu cross and were evidently fun little dogs. Their characters spoke from the pictures. However, when we met Wexford he was obviously a shadow of his former self, listless and without the spark that was so apparent in his portraits. Susan herself was in a state that combined high tension with high excitement. She was a bit like a cat on a hot tin roof. Her eagerness to find out whatever it was we had to reveal was matched by her trepidation at what it was that she would learn. There was also a slight time pressure because she was due to take Wexford to the vet in a couple of hours time, so with very little preamble I launched into a full explanation about animal reincarnation, channelling and the fact that Michael had told me that I could find Buddy for her.

In many ways Susan is like a female version of me. She's very practical, level headed and down to earth. But she is also open to the possibilities that are out there, so instead of rebutting the information we had given her, she just asked a barrage of questions.

In the meantime, Sharon had begun working on Wexford but found that whilst he appeared to enjoy the energies as they were being run in to him, he didn't actually need them. When she relayed this to the still worried Susan, Michael chipped in "There's nothing wrong with Wexford now. He volunteered to have this illness so that this meeting could take place. He is a signpost for you (Susan), and now that you have received this awakening, he no longer needs to be ill. If this meeting had taken place when the opportunity first arose, it would not have been necessary."

What is an awakening and what is a signpost?

The knowledge of what we truly are, our purpose in life and the learning that we are meant to accumulate across a lifetime is all lost to us at birth. Although it is we ourselves who have defined these things, it is a really good thing that we forget them because otherwise we would arrive weighed down with the burden of this knowledge and it would affect the way we live our lifetimes immeasurably. The concept of free will would be abandoned. Massive guilt could result.

However, as we live out our lifetimes we do want to make progress from soul level to soul level so we need to achieve at least some form of awakening to the information that we lose. As we progress across soul levels the extent of the awakening required increases on an exponential basis until it becomes total. We need to discover everything that we have forgotten.

During the planning process that we go through before incarnating, we schedule a number of events or encounters with people across our lifetimes who will act as signposts for us. These are intended to provoke this awakening to the extent that is required in that particular lifetime. If we don't understand their significance as they happen, others will be

---

scheduled for later on in life. Signposts tend to get progressively bigger and more obvious to make them more recognisable.

Anybody can be a signpost for anybody else and as is clear from Wexford's tale, even a dog can agree to be a signpost.

This is the way the whole process would work:

In transitioning between lifetimes, whilst in the form of our higher selves, Susan, Sharon, Wexford, Buddy and I would have reached an agreement. (Don't forget that animals in their true form are identical to us.)

The agreement would have been that I was to give Susan information about the true nature of her existence. This information would constitute her awakening.

To make this work, both Wexford and Buddy would have scheduled a lifetime with Susan.

Upon Buddy's passing, I was supposed to have spoken with her to reveal the information.

Because I didn't, which was foreseeable, the backup plan was that Wexford would become ill, prompting a visit at which point the information would be revealed.

But what if Buddy and Wexford had never got to Susan in the first place? What if Susan had not been Jenny's teacher? What if we had never moved to Canada? There are so many iterations of possibility that it is easy to see how flimsy a plan like this might appear!

However, you might recall what was said earlier on about what is predetermined? Major events in a lifetime are effectively cast in stone. In the context of signposts, their setting is quite rigid and they are only *ever* based upon certainties. It was an issue of absolute certainty that I would give the information to Susan at some point. In this context, it was also absolutely certain that Buddy and Wexford would come to live with Susan when they incarnated.

However, the issue of them returning to her was absolutely not certain and was a matter of choice for them. This will be explained later.

It is by no means the case that all dogs are signposts. Buddy and Wexford were involved in this way since it was predetermined that the nature of her relationship with them would be a key factor in making Susan sit up and take notice. There are many other possible signposts that could have brought Susan to her awakening, but the significance of the dogs to her meant that they would be a sure fire route to getting her attention.

The events surrounding Susan, Buddy and Wexford are by no means unique. In some respects they are typical of the way in which one thing leads to another in a seemingly unconnected fashion until a higher purpose is revealed. Signposts are extremely sophisticated in their apparent simplicity since it is that very feature that belies their massive degree of complexity.

Particularly for old souls, the time spent in planning and preparing for signposts is considered to be one of the most significant aspects of soul transitioning.

The way it worked in this case was that Buddy's death provoked what should have been a signpost meeting for Susan with me. It didn't happen because of the intervention of my free will. As with all things, free will can interfere with the way things come to pass.

This is very unlikely to have been Susan's first signpost. There could have been many previously that she had not noticed or ignored. Neither would it necessarily be her last. Depending on how much she took the information to heart, acted upon it and sought to discover its meaning, she might have more scheduled in future that could be of greater impact, or gentle reminders.

Once all of these concepts had been explained to Susan, she seemed a happier, if somewhat bemused person. So then I asked the sixty four thousand dollar question: "So, do you want me to try and find Buddy for you?" It was a total no brainer and I already knew the answer, but Michael said that I *had* to ask the question.

Why did I *have* to ask the question?

Just because I receive information about somebody, it doesn't mean that I have an automatic right to foist it upon them. Although Susan was certainly 'scheduled' to get the broader information about spiritual matters from us, whether or not she took Buddy back was still a matter of free will and choice. Therefore she actually had to request the information before I could give it to her.

Of course, I could have told her anyway, but that would have been contrary to her highest good and therefore contrary to the highest good of all.

Having received the answer I was then able to relay information that Michael had already given me: Buddy would not be returning as a cross breed dog. Next time around he would be a Highland Terrier. He would be a male.

Why wasn't Buddy going to come back as a cross breed?

On the balance of probabilities, the lives of pure bred dogs are more likely (although certainly not guaranteed) to be easier than mongrels.

If at this point you, as the owner of a cross breed, are upset by this statement, don't be. Think about it: Statistically it is a fact that the majority of dogs that get rehomed, abandoned, live lives as strays or get terminated in pounds are cross breeds. Few people actually buy a cross breed since their worth is not generally acknowledged, unless it is as a result of intentional creation of a new breed through cross breeding as is the case with Labradoodles (that now command a very high price). The risks that are inherent in a crossbreed lifetime are therefore many.

Pure bred dogs tend to be sold. Households that have invested their hard earned money in a dog tend to be more reticent about rejecting them since if nothing else, this would be the equivalent of throwing away money.

These comments bear no reflection on the huge number of homes that offer loving environments to crossbreed dogs, nor are they an endorsement of those that have purebreds. Both may be equally beneficial to the dog's development.

Irrespective of all of this, dog souls will undoubtedly incarnate as crossbreeds at some point in their development.

In this case Buddy was coming back as a specific breed because it would make him infinitely easier to find. Crossbreeding is seldom planned or the progeny advertised in the way that pure bred matings are.

If Buddy had returned as a crossbreed, it is immensely unlikely that I could have been led to him.

He was due to come back quite shortly, but if things didn't work out, he would be able to delay his incarnation to give Susan a good chance at recovering him.

How could Buddy delay his return?

The average time taken in linear terms for reincarnation to occur is six months, although from a different perspective, possibly hundreds of linear years will have passed before a soul returns.

Because of the specific reasoning behind Buddy's return (explained below), a somewhat less random approach to the timing of his return was enabled.

This may appear to be somewhat arbitrary in that one entity was able to make changes that had potentially cosmic significance. However, had this delay been unconscionable it would not have happened. Plus, Buddy's return also has significance for Susan's progression along her ascension pathway, and therefore it was highly desirable that his return be facilitated in a manner that was convenient for both of them.

It is not always the case that such allowances may be made. As a rule, once a reincarnation is scheduled, it goes ahead. In this instance a delay was actually brought about as a result of angels 'running interference'.

When I'd finished relaying all of this information Susan wore a stunned look on her face. "I always wanted a Highland Terrier" she said.

"Yes, Buddy knows that. He figured that was his best chance of getting back to you"

Despite the earlier reassurances, Susan was still nervous about Wexford. How long did he have left? Would he still be there when Buddy returned? How would they get on?

Michael was most emphatic: Wexford would make a full recovery. There was no reason why he could not go on for at least another two years, unless his higher self chose otherwise. He would definitely want to be there to be reunited with Buddy. He would recognise the new puppy as Buddy. Although the old dog would have the difficulties you would expect dealing with a young dog, they would nevertheless ultimately enjoy their reunification. And by the way, when he passed over, Wexford would also like to return to Susan. However, he intended to return as a Wheaten Terrier.

<u>Why did Buddy and Wexford want to return to Susan?</u>

The predetermined lifetime that this pair had lived with Susan had obviously served to enhance their own level of soul development. I am not fully aware of the circumstances so I cannot explain what specifically has come to pass between them. What I can report with certainty is that the synergy that exists between them prompts their desire. There is more learning that can be achieved within the relationship and warrants at least one further lifetime together for them all.

Once again, Susan was staggered by this information. "You know what" she said. "The second type of dog I always wanted was a Wheaten Terrier."

To me it was no surprise, but a very happy conclusion to what could have been a very awkward series of explanations. As we left, Wexford already seemed to have perked up and Sharon was very aware that his energy levels had soared.

All that now remained was for me to find precisely where Buddy would return and with angelic assistance this took a matter of minutes upon my return home. The breeder I was guided to didn't have any puppies at that point, or even any that were due. But Michael confirmed that it was definitely the right place so I emailed Susan with the information.

She replied immediately, again full of surprise: The kennel was in the same town that her parents lived in. And by the way, the vet had been very surprised by Wexford. Apparently, somewhat miraculously, he seemed to be well on the road to recovery. (No big surprise there!)

Susan took my advice about ensuring a place of precedence on the breeder's waiting list and that night she called them to ask about upcoming litters. Apparently demand was already very high but there would be a litter coming in about six months time. Because of her familiarity with the location, Susan chatted with the breeder for some time. Curiously enough, she chose to reveal to the breeder what we had told her about the puppy being Buddy's reincarnation. I'm not sure of the breeder's reaction but it was a very brave thing for Susan to do and I wondered if she was now, in turn, a signpost for the breeder.

The months rolled by and we became close friends with Susan. We discovered that we had a lot in common and have spent many happy hours in her company. On the next occasion that we saw her and Wexford, the little dog was clearly back on form and he is quite a joy to watch.

Then a few weeks ago, I received a frantic email from Susan. The puppies had been born and Susan had to pick a dog. The breeder had sent loads of pictures but which one was he? Help! Almost simultaneously, she rang. She needed an immediate answer because the number of available puppies was already limited. She didn't know from the photos which dogs were still available so he might already have been taken. I asked if Susan had a sense of which one it might be. She had, but she wouldn't tell me because she didn't want to influence me. I actually felt a sense of panic because it was so important that I find the right one and I asked for time to tune in and ensure that I was hearing correctly. But there was no time so I pointed out the one in a group photo I thought Michael was saying was Buddy. When Susan was off the line I tuned in and was relieved to find that I had indicated the right one.

However, it transpired that Susan was attracted to a puppy in another picture that she believed was Buddy. When she spoke to the breeder on the phone she asked about that one too. She was delighted to find that it was actually the same puppy and by the end of the day, the breeder had confirmed that Susan could have this dog.

To say that Susan was on cloud nine would be a hopeless understatement. By her own account and those we subsequently heard from Jenny and Shannon, she positively glowed for the next fortnight.

Do all dogs try to get back to their previous owners?

Absolutely not! It is a testament to Susan that Buddy and Wexford went to such great lengths to achieve this.

Unless they are part of the web of an individual's signposts dogs find themselves going to households on a random basis. As already stated, there is so much in their lives that is by chance that it is the equivalent of throwing themselves into the void. This is the lot of those light beings that incarnate as dogs and this is the way in which they are meant to learn.

However, whilst experiencing a lifetime with a particular family or human being, a dog's higher self might recognise that the experience of living with them presents opportunities for learning or even achieving balance. Under these circumstances, during their soul transitioning they might well try to orchestrate a return to that household. But if you consider all of the variables that come into play, unless the owner is directed to find them, the odds of being successful are at best slim.

It should also be acknowledged that a vast number of dogs have bitterly unpleasant experiences with their human owners. Under these circumstances they will not wish to return to that owner.

Whilst it is easy to condemn the actions of those who mistreat their animals, it should be recalled that the purpose of humans sharing their lives with pets is one which plays upon the learning synergies that can be created. A human that mistreats an animal has potentially created a learning opportunity for the creature; or vice-versa. It is sad but true that even in the most ghastly of experiences, great learning can be found. If it is achieved, there is no need to repeat the experience.

Even where a relationship has been synergistically successful, the animal will not necessarily want to return to the same human. It may have exhausted the learning opportunities that exist within that household.

I consider it likely that Sage only returned to us because a full lifetime in our household would be beneficial. I already know that several of our non-avatars will be reincarnating after they move on because they have not yet achieved balance and are unlikely to in this lifetime. But I don't believe that this group (or at least those you have heard about so far!) - Pippa, Emily, Daisy, Molly - will come back to us, even if we wanted to find them.

It's a hard fact to face, but all souls in their transitioning make choices in favour of their highest good, which is in turn for the highest good of all. It is an issue of personal mastery to accept that fact and not let our emotions concerning our pets rule our hearts. And that's tough.

Where our family is undoubtedly far more fortunate than most that lose their beloved pets is that Michael will let us know when the time comes and we will be certain about whether or not we should be trying to facilitate their return.

As I write this, it is one week since Buddy (or Jock, as he is now known) arrived back with Susan. Two days after his homecoming we were invited to come and visit with him, and he is one of the cutest puppies that I have seen.

Unfortunately my predictions about Wexford's reaction to him were accurate. The old dog did initially take umbrage with the younger one but even worse, the day before our meeting, Wexford got sick, demonstrating the same symptoms that Buddy had before he passed over. Panic stricken, Susan took him to the vet and although when we arrived, things had greatly improved, she was shaken and very worried that her action in bringing Buddy/Jock back into the house had actually precipitated the illness. Once again we were faced with a distraught woman on the verge of freefall panic and riddled with guilt. Inevitably it played on her mind that Wexford would now chose to go.

For a moment he did.

This was not because of the third dimensional reasons of hurt that Susan was ascribing to him. He did indeed recognise his fellow soul traveller and undoubtedly he experienced jealously that Buddy was now back in a young and agile body, whereas he was stuck in an old and relatively frail one with failing eyesight, kidney problems and an intolerance for proteins. In all likelihood he experienced pangs of envy that he was presented with a vibrant being that had its whole life ahead of it. And probably, he found the presence of a lively and inquisitive puppy just plain annoying.

However, the choice point was his higher self's. Recognising that it would be a more useful experience for Wexford to be reunited with Buddy in a younger form so as to continue their journey together as equals, and so enhance their learning, it toyed with the idea of pulling Wexford out. It could do this by simply allowing him to be overcome by existing physical ailments, and it began to do this.

Susan's reaction was powerful and agonised. She could not bear to lose Wexford, at least not now; and so his higher self altered its decision. It was a classic example of one being deferring its needs for the needs of another.

Sadly, one of the very few pictures we have of Sage. We thought we'd have so much more time.

Lara keeps a watchful eye on the world.

Ktuu and me, with both of us relishing her newly acquired fresh breath!

Cinnda thinks this new home is great if you can sit on sofas…

Timba in his first experience of snow is immediately an addict.

A fully grown Indy out for a casual 15km hike at the very top of a 2225m mountain.

Lara and Cinnda admiring the view with Sharon.

Joe adoring the attention he gets from Angie and Diego's daughter Valeria.

Indy and Kaiti after a winter hike. Kaiti needs the coat but Indy's just fine, even in minus 30c.

Saffy isn't scared, just permanently wide eyed.

Indy on a hike, coveting every mouthful of Sharon's lunch.

Ktuu is convinced that even a camera can hold some kind of food.

Lara turns out to be an excellent and very proud mother.

The whole family standing on a frozen Lake Louise, Christmas 2007 with Sage, Indy and Dougal. We lost Sage 5 days later.

The puppies get a new sibling: Zoe, Aura, Inara and Sheepy.

Timba struggles to accept that the packet of crackers really is empty.

On a crystal planting hike, Cinnda is fascinated with Garry's anointing of a huge piece of rose quartz.

The puppies start to take an interest in the world. (Idaho, Inara, Zoe, Aura.)

Indy cutting a fine figure at more than half Sharon's height.

The mysterious and stunning Kachina, about whom more will be written.

Angelic interventions: Sage's tale (Part II)

Shortly after we had met Susan, we got an email to let us know that Sage's new mother had conceived.

The news came in the same week that Lara was due to have her operation to be spayed. The night before the surgery it snowed heavily and as I looked out of the window, I noticed Tristan struggling with the gate as he tried to get out to board the school bus. I went down to help and found the snow piled so high that it was impossible to open the gate more than a few inches. Tristan squeezed through but I would not be able to get the car out to take Lara to the vet. It was lucky that I had noticed this now. Fifteen minutes later I had shovelled away enough of the white stuff to be able to open the gate wide enough for the car to pass and I went to the garage to return the shovel and unplug the block heater from the car. It was then that I noticed that it was listing over at a peculiar angle. I groaned when I saw that we had a flat tire on our rear passenger side wheel, and realising that we would be late for taking Lara to the vets, I hurriedly set about changing the tyre in the freezing cold.

As I was doing so the phone in the garage rang. I was too preoccupied to answer and besides, somebody else in the house would pick it up. I was just finishing off tightening the wheel nuts when Sharon entered through the door that led to the house. She had been unaware of the puncture, so she was probably coming to find out why I was taking so long to get ready. Instead, she greeted me with the news that the surgery was off because the vet's wife had gone into labour that morning and all appointments were cancelled.

I was suddenly struck by the fact that there had now been three events in a row that could have, and eventually did prevent us from taking Lara for the operation, just like the three ratifications in the physical that I would request for things I was uncertain of. Immediately I asked Michael what was going on.

"The avatar does not want to have the operation yet" he said. Again, it was one of those moments when I sensed I was experiencing a tantalising glimpse of a bigger purpose at work, but when I asked "Why not?" he simply said: "Because she is not yet ready for this experience". I accepted that and told Sharon why the operation was really off. It seemed obvious so we thought no more of it and decided that we'd ask next time we arranged an operation so that the universe would not have to go to such trouble to prevent it.

Just over two months later we received a very brief email to give us the happy news that Sage's new mother had delivered a litter of three puppies, one of which was supposed to be Sage's reincarnation. Full details were to follow. Because of the nature of her return, we had already decided that she would be called Anastasia, which in Russian means 'resurrection'. We met the news of the birth with great anticipation and excitement. But just over twenty four hours later, the breeder sent us the shocking news that all of the puppies were boys.

We were flabbergasted! How could this be? Immediately I tuned in and demanded an explanation. What had happened to Sage since she clearly wasn't one of the new puppies? "Why did you assume that she would return as a female?" Michael replied. "As with all forms, the issue of sex is a matter of learning and in this incarnation it is convenient for her to be a male." I relayed the information to Sharon and once again we were embarrassed by the assumptions we had made. We had not asked enough questions and we had not asked the right questions, although for a brief moment it occurred to me that Michael had simply been obtuse in his revelations.

Was Michael being obtuse?

It is actually quite usual for angels to communicate in a way that appears incomplete or evasive. This is because of the limitations of the parameters within which they are allowed to intervene in our lives.

Firstly there is a limit to how much information they are able to give us because if they stray beyond this, they risk affecting the extent to which we will then exercise our own free will.

Mainly this relates to the extent to which they will provide information about the future. This is strictly forbidden since once somebody has an idea of what their future *should* be they will then alter the use of their free will to try and make that future happen (or not happen).

The utilisation of our free will and our ability to choose is part of our purpose for being here in the first place, so angels will do nothing to subvert this.

Secondly, there is the issue of how they communicate from a broader perspective. The vast majority of angels, particularly Archangels, have never walked the planet. Neither are they omniscient. They are not fully aware of the nuances and subtleties of our communications and when they respond to what they are asked, they do not second-guess what the questioner is really saying, they take the questions at a literal level and respond accordingly.

Thirdly there is an issue of timing. Certain information you need to know at the time when it is right to know and not beforehand. This is because of the way in which the newfound knowledge will affect you.

There is a degree to which angels have discretion on these points but the parameters are not very broad.

Because I hadn't *asked* if Sage was coming back as a female, he saw no reason to share this information, particularly as it might have altered our choices in a moment when we were already receiving privileged information.

An angel can never lie to you. They can never deceive you. But facts may be omitted either for your own highest good or because you simply did not ask the right question.

Then finally the penny dropped and I half laughed and half choked. The glimpse of the bigger purpose that I had seen two months previously on the morning Lara was supposed to be spayed came suddenly and starkly into focus.

Not only had we not received the complete explanation of why Lara didn't want to have the operation at that point, we had also never fully

191

pursued our understanding of the relationship that she desired with the reincarnated Sage when she returned to us. Again we had succumbed to assumptions. Now I knew:

"The Lara avatar wants to have puppies by Sage's reincarnation. She wants to experience childbirth and motherhood. Lara knew Sage was coming back as a male dog all along." I blurted out. Sharon's jaw dropped and Michael said "Yes", as if I should have grasped that all along.

"Oh my God" was all Sharon could manage.

The puppy stage of a dog's life is probably the most difficult for the owners. The constant need they have for attention and watchfulness, the indiscriminate use of the house as a toilet facility, the propensity for damaging anything and everything; all of these factors contribute towards making puppyhood a few months of nightmare. Sure, they're cute and cuddly and lovable and fun to watch. But many households actually reject dogs at this stage of their lives just because they can be so needy and destructive. And even we, now consummate dog people, had it in our minds that we could only ever cope with one puppy at a time. We had never dreamed of any of our dogs having puppies. We followed all the right practices to ensure that we never would be proud grandparents! All of our dogs were neutered.

"At least three of the puppies will be avatars" Michael added.

OK we thought, that's a privilege, but as we were now starting to wise up to the need to be a little more effective with our questioning techniques we needed to know why?

"It is necessary for the energy line" he added, and we left it at that.

It took a little while to adjust. The implications of having puppies gradually began to sink in and we were moderately consoled by the knowledge that Huskies usually have small litters. We totally missed the implications of the words "At least three of the puppies..."

From that point onwards, Sage/Anastasia needed a new name. And that is why this tale now needs to become Timbaland's tale.

We had already chosen Timbaland's name before we saw the picture of him. His full name is actually Mr Timbaland, and yes, he was named after the rapper. We quickly abbreviated the name to Timba.

Ultimately, after the new knowledge Michael had imparted had filtered through, we were quite relaxed about Sage coming back as a boy. The issue of the puppies was too far off for us to worry about since Lara was still only young and we envisaged her having the puppies in a few years time. So there was no point in worrying about that now.

I still harboured minor concerns about choosing the right puppy, but when the photos came, despite the fact that the three puppies were very similar, the one that was Sage almost leapt off the computer screen at me. Michael confirmed my selection and since, as you may recall, I was top of the waiting list, I had no doubt that we would get her. So I emailed the breeder with our choice and we sat back to wait for his arrival.

However, the next day we received an email from the breeder, apologising for the misunderstanding and explaining that we did indeed have first choice, but only after the owners of the puppies' parents had theirs. Somewhat strangely it also seemed that neither of the dogs was hers. In other words, we now had a one in three chance of getting Sage back and if someone else took a fancy to our choice of puppy, she was gone forever.

I found this news very disturbing and immediately asked Michael if he could intervene. All he would say was that they would try to influence the choices of the owners but freedom of choice could not be denied. It was an unassailable right.

Three weeks passed whilst we were on tenterhooks. Then finally we got an email from the breeder. The owners had made their choices and we could have the puppy that we wanted. Furthermore, in her opinion we were getting the pick of the litter and she even seemed a bit surprised that we were getting this particular puppy. I asked Michael what had happened and got a curious reply: "We may not intervene in the exercise of freewill, but we may run interference".

<u>What does 'running interference' mean?</u>

Although our rights of freedom of choice and freewill are unassailable, the circumstances that surround us may be altered and influenced by those in the etheric realms.

What we see and perceive may be altered so that our responses to situations change.

This is a reasonably regular occurrence so that things that are 'meant to be' (i.e. those things which are pre-ordained for the highest good) come about.

In this specific instance, when those who were entitled to first choice of dog looked at Timba, they saw something quite different from his true appearance.

So effectively they made their choices of their own volition and were undoubtedly happy with them. But the data that they used to make the choice was somewhat distorted by the angels so that he would come to us.

Wow!!

However it came about, we were delighted that it had happened that way and I could barely stop myself from cheering. Then I read on in the email: The breeder hoped that I wouldn't mind but he had registered the puppies with the Canadian Kennel Club and he had named our puppy. This didn't affect what we called him at all, but it would be his registered name. The kennel was called Alantra and the puppy had been registered as Alantra's Meant To Be.

And so it was!

Buy one, get one free: Cinnda and Ktuu's tale

My memory is generally regarded as astounding by those who know me, so it is a very odd thing when I cannot remember why something happened, yet I have no idea why, at the end of June 2008, in the lead up to Timba's pending arrival, I was looking at Husky rescue sites on the internet.

I was reading some of the appalling tales of the fates that had overtaken these dogs that now found themselves in need of new homes. Many had been pulled out of high kill shelters, saved at the eleventh hour; others had been dumped without ceremony by owners who no longer wanted them; a surprising few were just strays. Often they were the subject of abuse and unspeakable cruelty that had affected their personalities. Many had medical conditions that would make them undesirable. A great number were simply too old to be of interest to potential owners. Reading the stories was grim and heartbreaking, yet at least they were still alive and something compelled me to read about them.

After some time I found myself on the website of Athabasca Husky rescue. The site had videos that accompanied the descriptions of some of the dogs and my attention was drawn to a rather shy and quiet Siberian Husky that had apparently once been a lead sled dog. One day she had decided that she didn't like snow or dirt or cold, so now they were seeking a new home for her. She didn't have the grim tale of many other dogs, in fact she had been cherished by her owner. But for a working sled kennel, she now served little purpose and was simply a mouth to feed that did not pay for itself. Basic economics did not tolerate that. As I watched her on the video it dawned on me that I was looking at an avatar and this was confirmed by Michael. Then came the inevitable: "There would be benefit in rescuing this dog."

I called Sharon and showed her the dog but our attention was also drawn to another dog. This one was an Alaskan Malamute. Seeing her on video she could best be described as 'goofy'. She came from another sled team but the owners had been killed and this dog, along with dozens of others from the kennel, needed to be rehomed. Other sled

195

team owners from the area had come and picked out dogs they thought would be of value to their teams, but this one had been ignored by all. She was very old and had spinal issues as well as major problems with her teeth. "Is she an avatar too?" asked Sharon. Michael replied that she wasn't and he offered no recommendation whatsoever other than to say that it would be an "act of kindness" if we took her. We tried to find out more information but little was forthcoming.

Why wouldn't Michael tell us more?

There comes a point beyond which the information that we are given can start to affect our freedom of choice. When Michael gives the bare minimum like this it is because our decisions would likely change if the whole story were to be revealed.

This can be frustrating; but as in this case, had we known what he meant we would most definitely have felt obliged to help the dog.

As it was, with so little to go on, we acted entirely upon our own free will.

Those who have never done it will not necessarily appreciate that the process of adopting a rescue dog is actually far trickier than buying a dog. Previous accounts of Dougal and Daisy may have seemed easy or even casual, but this is only because we were taking them from a breeder and she already knew us well.

If you take a dog from a rescue then you have to provide considerable information about yourself and the vetting process will usually involve a house visit. Essentially, the shelter needs to get as much assurance as possible that the dog you adopt will not go through a repeat performance of the emotional hardships they have already undergone. It is a common and short-sighted misconception that dogs in shelters are strays that have brought their circumstances upon themselves. It is far more common that they have been 'dumped' or given up when they are no longer wanted.

Dogs that need to be rehomed are often traumatised by their experiences, having been ripped away from their familiar settings. Many have been mistreated and are deeply mistrustful. The people who work in animal shelters mostly do so on a voluntary basis. They provide sensitive and loving care for these damaged creatures and a great deal of the role that they perform is one of rehabilitation. Having once established such a relationship with the animal, they are then very keen to ensure that the good work done is not wasted; but more importantly that there is no further suffering.

When we took Sage we went through the vetting process and now this was repeated on behalf of the two dogs that we were interested in. After a great deal of correspondence and numerous telephone conversations, the lady who ran the shelter agreed that we *might* be good prospective owners for the pair, but she still reserved the right to not let us have the dogs. Therefore, whilst all seemed to be good, we would still have to take the risk of driving the fourteen hour round trip, plus overnight stay, of our own accord. This didn't concern us but we were interested, after all of the information that she now had about us, what other possible criteria could now be used to assess us?

That weekend we set off and drove north for five hours. We passed a very pleasant night in a hotel before rising early to complete the remaining two hours of the journey, and we arrived at the rescue centre in the mid morning. It was the first time we had visited such a place and we were totally taken by surprise. There were dogs everywhere. This sanctuary housed over fifty misplaced Huskies and Malamutes and the 'talking' as we drove up was incredible. We were soon being given a guided tour and told the stories of many of these fascinating animals. Included amongst them were three wolf-hybrids. They were remarkable to look at and when approached, they would regard you for a few moments, apparently deciding whether or not you were a risk. After that they were surprisingly friendly. The way they looked at you is something that I will never forget since they almost seemed to be looking into your soul.

After the tour we took the two potential rescues for a walk and got on well with them as we fussed with them and talked to the lady who ran the centre. She seemed anxious to point out to us that Ktuu was a very

197

old lady with maybe not too much time left. She desperately wanted her to go to a home where she would spend her last days being loved and accepted. Part of her was clearly surprised but also delighted that we would even consider taking such an old dog.

I asked what more she needed to do to assess our suitability. "Oh, that's already done" she explained. "Every time I have a potential owner visit I introduce them to the wolves. One in particular is very choosy about who she will let into her space. I trust her judgement completely and if she didn't like you, there's no way I'd let you take one of my dogs". We had passed the wolf test without any problems at all, so we were OK, but what about others I wondered? "Well, she actually rejects about one in six people" came the reply.

I found this process of vetting intriguing and I would have loved to have spent more time with the hybrids. Whilst I would never own one (and the methods used to breed them are often deeply disturbing) they were breathtaking creatures.

How did the wolf hybrids know we were OK?

The wolves apparently assessed us on the basis of smell.

In actual fact they were using their noses as receptors for picking up the vibrations created by our thoughts which in turn revealed our intentions. Even if we had tried to hide them, they would have been able to pick them up.

I asked Michael how effective the vetting process would be and he assured me that it was one hundred percent accurate. The wolf hybrids almost literally *could* see into our souls!

We tend to view animals as dumb creatures that are inferior to us in all aspects apart from those that are related to physical prowess. In the area of intelligence we certainly dismiss them as being far below our equal. Yet we do not fully comprehend all that they are capable of and we never acknowledge that in their light being form, they are identical to us.

When the time came to leave and make payment for the dogs, the lady only charged us for one dog. She certainly needed the money to help out with the very high costs of supporting so many dogs. However, she insisted that she was so glad to see Ktuu go to a loving home that there would be no charge. It felt a bit like a 'buy one, get one free' bargain and although we felt a little guilty, we were delighted since we couldn't really afford to take both dogs.

Why did we have to pay for a 'second hand' dog?

A lot of people seem to find it surprising that rescue dogs cost anything at all.

In actual fact, dogs that have ended up in rescue very often have to have a great deal of money spent on them before they can be rehomed.

If they have experienced abuse, this may have left them injured. Many are abandoned because they are sick and require expensive treatment which their owners are not prepared to pay for. But even if they are healthy, they still have to be fed and housed and looked after. All this costs a great deal of money.

Most shelters can only exist as a result of the donations they receive and the selflessness of the individuals who run them. They ask for donations (which vary in amount depending upon the shelter) to try to recoup at least some of the expenses.

To contribute to these costs was the very least we could do.

It took us another seven hours to drive home but the dogs were good travellers. Having both been outdoor dogs, they initially seemed to regard the house with some suspicion, but once inside, they both settled very quickly and the problem then became how to persuade them that if they went outside, we would let them come back in again.

In sniffing around the house Cinnda concluded that the ultimate best place to be was on a leather couch in the lounge. I took a picture of her whilst she was there because of the expression of pure pleasure that spread over her face after she got up. Sadly for her, she was a bit too big to be accorded the same privileges as Daisy or Briony. Having been put off the sofa, she established a favoured place on a bed in the 'wet room' beside the laundry and made this her home.

Having been a lead sled dog we had anticipated that she would be somewhat dominant and maybe even aggressive towards the others as a result; but we couldn't have been more wrong. She is very much an omega dog, placid, calm and very tolerant of the others. For the majority of the time she prefers to keep to herself and stays on her bed. Then she will have moments of wild abandon when she plays with the others and races around the fenced enclosure like a racehorse. None of the others is able to catch her. It is a source of minor sadness to us that she misses out on some of the pack activity because whenever the whole family is in the basement, she will not come downstairs. She appears to have a pathological fear of stairs and although if you pick her up and put her down halfway, she copes with no problems at all, she will not go either up or down of her own volition.

We soon discovered that Ktuu had major problems. We had already noticed that she moved slowly with a stiffness and gait that betrayed pain or damage in her lower spine. We figured it was most likely that she had been one of the dogs nearest to the sled in her team and had thus taken a great deal of the weight involved in the initial pull. We read reports that years of having to do this could leave the dog crippled with arthritis or issues within the spinal column itself. Our immediate response was to put a magnetic collar on her to see if its field could help relieve her pain in the same way that it had done for Pippa. Ktuu also hung her head and was painfully thin. We took the thinness to be a result of her previous circumstances and were confident that we would soon supply her with enough food to put some covering flesh on her. But worst of all was her breath. To describe it as rank would be a massive understatement. I cannot recall ever having experienced anything as foul and unpleasant as having Ktuu breathe on you. It was as if something had gotten into her mouth and died there a long time ago. It was definitely a rotting smell. To make matters worse, she was one of those dogs who liked to put her face near yours.

200

Within two days it became apparent that the breath, the hanging of the head and the weight issues were all connected. Her teeth were in such appalling condition that she could not eat. It was her teeth and gums that smelt and the hanging of the head was as a result of being in pain. A visit to our vet confirmed that things were even worse than we thought. She was admitted for surgery immediately and it was discovered that her mouth was a mass of cysts and ulcers, many of which were under her teeth and inside the gums. In a three hour operation she had nine of the offending articles removed and numerous puss drainages were carried out. The operation repeatedly had to be stopped because the smell was so overpowering. The gums were in such appalling condition that the resulting holes could not be sown up. The vet telephoned to let us know the news and that night when we went to collect her, we anticipated a dog that would be in an even worse state as a result of this intense procedure.

We were shocked by what we found: Ktuu was like a little puppy. Her head was held up and she greeted us with manic affection. There was no evidence of anything other than relief as she skipped merrily out of the office and when we got home, she even wanted food. From that point on we had a different dog living with us and we were delighted to be able to tell the rescue centre of this transformation. Within days she was eating like one of the other dogs, despite only having about six teeth left; the magnetic collar began to work its wonders and she began to play with the other dogs. It seemed clear why Michael had said that to take her would be an act of kindness since without the surgery, it is likely that she would have wasted away to nothing.

The only remaining problem was her sleeping. She was obviously unused to dog beds and refused them. At night she would wander around on the mid level because like Cinnda, stairs seemed to hold fear. Then one night she sat at the bottom of the flight that leads to the bedrooms, looking wistfully up at the retreating humans. After a few seconds she leapt up them three at a time as if she were a mountain goat. And since then, she has slept on the floor at Sharon's side.

Over the coming months both Cinnda and Ktuu put on some essential weight. You can no longer feel the sharp relief of Ktuu's spine and the obvious pain that she used to experience is thankfully absent. To see her run is an awe inspiring sight since she moves with grace and a majestic quality that totally belies her age. We are convinced that she is regressing in years as her eyes seem clearer and she is as playful as a dog half her age.

However, we were wrong about why it would be an act of kindness to take her. One morning Michael revealed to us that being in our home had allowed her to come into balance and if she remains this way, she will ascend upon her transition. We just hope it doesn't come too soon.

The arrival of the energy line

Within days of Cinnda and Ktuu's arrival we began to notice that the energies around the house were shifting again and we were somewhat surprised to find that the energy line was no longer on the other side of the road but at the gateway at the end of our drive.

Naturally, we wanted to know what was going on and were told that because we now had so many avatars in our house that the line had been moving towards us for the past year, we just hadn't noticed. Of even greater significance was the fact that within three weeks it would pass right through the house.

By now information of this magnitude had sort of become second nature and we weren't at all perturbed. When your world transforms to the extent to which ours had over the past five years, it was not a major surprise.

Our laid back approach to the information was not something Michael condoned. Its coming was: "something we needed to be prepared for" he advised. We were already aware that the line had the power to 'move people on'; we knew that this happened because their energies were incompatible with the forces within the line, but we still hadn't explored any potential affects upon us. We were blissfully happy where we were and so it seemed obvious that we must be compatible with it.

Again, our egos took a beating when Michael explained that our ability to cope was in no small part due to the presence of Indy in our household. His purpose as an avatar was to anchor us in the place where we lived and thus far he had done so by absorbing all of the energetic affects that would otherwise have been unsettling for us. He had been with us since our third week of occupancy, and had he not been so, our stay might have been somewhat less comfortable. He would continue to do so until we managed to raise our vibrations to the point where we could cope, but until that time, Indy was the one who had to deal with the roller coaster ride affects of the energies. And it was not easy for him. When I heard this, I was as humbled as I had been with the revelations about Dougal. It also made understanding him a lot easier.

Now the energy line was about to actually go through our house and even Indy's presence could not assuage the assault that this would represent! Michael explained that the line was a very pure form of 'Creator light energy'. It resonated with a frequency of vibration that was very high and if our vibrations were not also raised to match or at least be somewhere approaching that of the line, its affect would be very disruptive. "In what way?" we wondered. "In just about every way possible" was the reply. It would have the effect of producing amplification of everything that we experienced in our lives to potentially outrageous levels. A simple sneeze could become pneumonia; a stomach ache, dysentery. A minor disagreement between Sharon and I would seem like a cause for divorce; irritation with the children, blind fury. A slightly peculiar dream would be an unstoppable nightmare; a fleeting negative thought could bring about catastrophe within our lives.

To say that this was intimidating would be something of an understatement. It was horrifying and we were desperate to know how we could possibly avoid these chilling eventualities. Michael was very quick to allay our fears. Our success at being unaffected by the already close proximity of the line was as a result of the fact that we had already raised our vibrations. We had managed this because of the level of balance that we had achieved in our lives; we just needed to raise it a little higher. The full import of this explanation passed me by at the time and for the umpteenth time, we assumed that we understood exactly what he meant.

Despite our best attempts to do as Michael had recommended, when the energy line finally arrived we all experienced the impact of the line relative to our own areas of imbalance. Tristan had weeks of sleeplessness and physical turbulence. Jenny was tortured in her relationships both at school and at home. Sharon and I bickered like little children over the pettiest of things. It was like riding a rollercoaster. We were not the only ones to feel the effects since the line repositioning to pass through our house meant that it was also considerably closer to Scott and Shannon's house. Having only been married for a year at this point, it also caused considerable turbulence for them and we found ourselves feeling that we should be apologising for having indirectly caused this effect. As it was, it helped that we were able to explain what was happening since once they had a context for the extraordinary strength of their feelings, it made it easier to cope with what they too were going through.

The only one amongst us who seemed to take nothing but pleasure from the line was Kaiti. The day it arrived, Kaiti insisted that she would sleep outside. Up until that point she was very firmly an indoor dog. Most of her day was spent indoors and although she loves to go for a walk, she is always happy to get back inside. It therefore came as a great shock that she was scratching at the door to get out late at night. I let her out thinking that this was simply a toilet need, but she did not return. An hour later I went out to find her and there she was, sitting quite happily on the front porch with no interest in coming in. From that point onwards up until the weather became too cold to spend the night there, Kaiti slept outside. Sometimes we would find her in the igloo shaped kennel we have (called a dogloo); at other times she would be sitting somewhere else, clearly basking in the energy. When we asked Michael about it he let us know that she resonated totally with the energy. She found it wholly nurturing.

In the still of the night, the new energy was most palpable. The intensity was extraordinary but also exciting. Those who are energetically sensitive can feel the energy as soon as they arrive. However it is most easily experienced walking towards it.

Then about a month after it had arrived, everything became extraordinarily calm. We had ridden out the storm and managed to become at least partially resonant with the line's energy. Once we had become used to it, the effect of the line was almost ambient and it was only on the odd nights when I took a stroll outside that I was aware of it.

One night after we had been hiking I was relaxing in the hot tub under the stars. As the water eased away the pains of the day, I gazed around me, marvelling as I always do at the wonderful sense of being at one with nature. The tops of the pine trees surrounding the house were swaying gently in the night breeze and the stars twinkled with a

205

brilliance that only a crystal clear sky will allow. Then I began to notice what appeared to be a disturbance about twenty feet up in the air. The best way to describe it would be to say that it looked like there was a thick but transparent clothes line suspended there, from which were hung vertical lines every two feet along that pointed towards the earth, falling for a few feet before becoming invisible. I watched this illusion for a long while, wondering if my eyes were deceiving me.

The next day Sharon would berate me for not having woken her. Despite her great fatigue after our walk, she was extremely disappointed not to have seen the vision that I saw, for this, Michael revealed, was the energy line.

The reincarnation: Timba's tale II

It was only one week after we collected Cinnda and Ktuu that Timba arrived from the opposite side of the country. He was flown in on a five hour flight and it was with irony that we realised we were collecting him from exactly the same place from which we had fetched Sage seven months previously.

Prior to his arrival we had corresponded at some length with the breeder to ensure that his journey would be as smooth as possible. It was obvious that the breeder's family had grown quite fond of the dog and from their perspective at least, even if he was not the puppy most likely to go on and be a show champion, he was certainly the nicest member of the litter. They spoke in glowing terms about his gentle and loving temperament and made us promise to give them regular updates on his progress.

The firebrand that we collected did not meet this description at all. Michael had warned us that upon her return, Sage would bring in as much of her light energy as possible and that as a result, the puppy would be headstrong and require strong leadership. But we hadn't expected anything like this.

What does it mean to bring in 'light energy'?

When we leave our higher selves to incarnate we have the opportunity to bring in a quantity of the light energy that our higher self is made up of. The energy gives us power.

How much we bring in with us will have a significant effect upon our lives because it will relate very closely to our ability to manifest. Broadly speaking, the more we have, the easier our lives will be.

However, the energy that we possess in itself provides a learning opportunity for us because its management and appropriate utilisation are not easy. Energy is power and power can easily be abused. Understanding this and learning to use it wisely and for the highest good

---

of all is one of the challenges that must be met and conquered across our lifetimes.

Young soul lifetimes are the phase of development during which we humans tend to bring in most light energy. (This is partially in compensation for the hardships of having been a baby soul). Its mastery can be illusive, which is the main reason we go through so many young soul lifetimes. By the time we get to being old souls, we bring in very little light energy.

Animals do not seem to follow the same sequence or logic. In Timba's case he brought so much with him so as to provide himself with a substantial challenge prior to ascension; but this will be dealt with shortly.

In sympathy for his uncomfortable and tedious journey we decided that we would let him out of the crate and that Sharon would have him on her lap, just as Jenny had done with Briony eighteen months earlier. Whereas the Poodle had sat nicely and licked Jenny in pure delight, Timba wriggled and nipped and chewed and whined. By the time we'd got half way home, he was driving us both crazy with his insane energy and apparently obstinate temperament. Finally we pulled over and re-crated him which merely served to fuel his anger.

When we finally arrived home and released him, instead of greeting the other dogs in the polite and interested manner that had been the feature of every single introduction we had previously made, he tried to bite anyone who came near him. He growled and prowled around and we were quite concerned that a fight would break out at any moment. As it was already late we put him to bed with a couple of the others in the wet room where he howled for a long time.

Clearly one of two things had happened: either they'd sent us the wrong dog and this wasn't Sage at all or the effect of bringing in so much energy meant that we were now sharing our house with the puppy from hell!

The next morning when I went to let the dogs out, a cute and friendly puppy greeted me in the wet room. He licked my hand and wagged his tail in a friendly manner. He went outside with the others and played nicely. He was gentle and sweet and everything that the breeder had promised he would be. It appeared that the stress of the journey had been very great and that he had arrived like an over wound clockwork toy. We were more than a little relieved.

Timba grew very quickly into a large and handsome dog. He is immensely strong and has a broad strong back with a saddle that always reminds me of a silverback gorilla! I have no doubt that he would be an excellent sled dog although he has not been trained to pull and walks quite nicely on a leash.

Somewhat surprisingly, he rapidly became best friends with Indy. Our 'gentle giant' is none too fond of other males and he has had several confrontations with Dougal in his attempt to become alpha dog. For some reason he accepts Timba totally and they frequently 'hang-out' together. Timba's favourite playmate is Briony, and they will spend hours play fighting, rising up on their hind legs and doing battle like a pair of creatures depicted in heraldic symbols. When it comes to relaxation, Timba prefers to chill out on the deck next to his big buddy and they are often to be seen strolling casually around the grounds together. As I write this, they are lying fast asleep, head to toe, by my side.

A question we are often asked by those who know the story is: "Can you tell that he's Sage?" When we first saw him, her spirit was obvious in the eyes and the puppy pictures were very obviously her, at least from our perspective. When we first took delivery of him, despite his attitude, you could tell it was her. Now, there's little resemblance and no sense of her energetically either, but this is to be expected.

Why can we no longer 'sense' Sage in Timba?

All babies are born with a strong connection with that which they have previously been. As such, it is possible to recognise them, but only for a brief period. In much the same way as we lose our soul memories by

209

necessity after we are born, any trace of our previous vibration is also likely to vanish. This is because the soul, in order to experience the uniqueness of the new incarnation must separate itself from what it has already gone through.

This is not to say that physical similarities will not present themselves from one incarnation to another. Some humans spontaneously remember whole lifetimes, often to their discomfiture due to their current circumstances. Perhaps dogs do the same.

Soul memories for humans may also be remembered spontaneously or by design through past life regression via hypnosis. This is only of value if an individual needs to know what has happened in a past life.

Physically their coats are very unalike and temperamentally Timba is in some respects an opposite of Sage. Specifically, he is unusually affectionate for a Husky and actively seeks out attention. He is polite and respectful whilst waiting for food and responds to basic commands without having received any training. As an issue of trying to achieve balance in this lifetime, Timba does the things that Sage's circumstances prevented her from doing.

Despite my certainty of Timba's origins, a few months into our ownership of him, the loss of the ability to recognise Sage began to trouble me. I was beginning to experience despondency and then an event occurred that was completely reassuring:

In her time with us, Sage showed that she was a dog of considerable intelligence. One of her unique behaviours stemmed from an understanding that if she placed a paw in her bowl whilst she was eating, the bowl would not move. Whilst the others would chase theirs around the slippery kitchen floor in the frustration of trying to get at their last morsel of food, she would stand still with her paw in the bowl and clean it out with precious little effort. I have never seen another dog do this.

Shortly after I began to have concerns about recognising her, Timba put his paw in his bowl and held it down as he ate. As he was doing so he turned and looked at me with the most knowing look I have ever seen in a dog. He has never repeated this action. But he does respond if you call him Sage.

Of course the most important relationship for Timba was that with his potential mate Lara. We never considered for one moment that they might not like each other and sure enough, they played together like brother and sister. However, Timba was soon much bigger and stronger than Lara and could be a little rough for her liking, so that was the point at which he turned his attentions to the (surprisingly) tougher Briony.

However, as soon as Lara came into season, he once again found her remarkably attractive and his rather more gentle attentions involved trailing after her wistfully with a silly love struck expression on his face. We weren't too concerned about her getting pregnant at this stage because Timba was still too young to be capable of fathering children; so we didn't keep them apart.

Besides, we didn't *need* to have the puppies yet, did we?

212

Managing the pack energies

If you're keeping count, we were now at the stage of having twelve dogs in the house, six of whom were avatars and three of whom were males. The energies in the house were phenomenal since each one of them provided a total contrast with the others and they varied in range from Kaiti's serenity through to Timba's youthful frenzy.

One of the things that we are most frequently asked is how we manage to control the chaos of a household with so many dogs. The answer is simple if a little confusing to the uninitiated: Cesar Milan.

Controlling the energies of a single dog can be too much for many people. The mistakes that 'parents' of canines often make have a lot to do with their ignorance of their dog's expectations of them. All too easily an animal that does not respect its master can become troublesome and the lives of all made a misery. We too could easily have fallen into this trap had we not seen Cesar Milan's show 'The Dog Whisperer' on the Discovery Channel whilst we were still in the UK.

If you have never seen it, you are missing a treat: The basic format of the program is that Cesar visits with three different dog owners during a show. He usually finds himself dealing with nightmare situations and seemingly untrainable canines of all sizes and temperaments. Sometimes he takes the problem dogs to his rescue sanctuary that specialises in helping the most aggressive dogs whose only other alternative would be euthanasia.

Often he is assisted by Daddy, a pit bull terrier who was once the property of the rap artist Redman, but was entrusted to Cesar when he was four months old. Cesar involves Daddy because of his calming energies and the impact that he creates on the other dogs. Both human and dog are truly role models. The program is always immensely entertaining but even more importantly, it imparts vast amounts of practical information that can greatly assist dog owners if they follow his teachings.

We first came across The Dog Whisperer a few years before we moved to Canada and using his techniques, found that we were able to deal with our dogs in a far simpler and calmer manner than previously. As the pack grew we followed his techniques and we have always found that some of the golden rules he imparts have proved essential in our ability to maintain order.

Cesar himself is in many ways a remarkable man. He has an instinctive understanding of the canine world which has given him an innate ability to deal with the most difficult of dogs and earn their respect and trust. He does this without ego or judgement of those whom he helps, despite the obvious deficiencies in dog ownership that he encounters. What he doesn't necessarily realise is the extent to which his teachings are fully in line with broader learning relating to the ascension pathway.

We had been enthusiastic viewers of the show for some while when Sharon decided to ask Michael about Daddy. Despite his intimidating appearance, Daddy is usually the picture of control and decorum. He is the very essence of a balanced dog and undoubtedly his presence enables Cesar to achieve and illustrate required techniques and behaviours with a greater degree of ease than he might otherwise have been able to. So when Michael explained that he was actually an avatar, it came to us as no shock whatsoever.

Michael went on to reveal that Daddy's purpose is to provide enlightenment for viewers about states of being since he deports himself with so much calm and controlled balance. He is a fine emissary, not only for a much misunderstood breed but for dogs in general. He is also singularly rare in that of all animals that make it into the media's eye, he is the *only* fully conscious avatar. I am fascinated, although not surprised, by the fact that when I have studied pictures of Daddy, looking into his eyes I see exactly the same essence of being looking back at me as when I closely study Kaiti.

Even more importantly, Daddy has provided learning for Cesar too. He was originally given to Cesar for fostering, but his pathway would always have taken him, one way or another, to Cesar's door. Although Cesar can boast of a huge number of success stories, I am convinced that he has been influenced by Daddy in much the same subtle way that Kaiti was able to impact upon us.

The language that is used in the show regularly makes reference to energies, balance and states of being. It constantly encourages and reinforces the need for a heightening of understanding between humans and the animal kingdom. And whilst it never comes anywhere close to espousing a set of spiritual beliefs (since this would undoubtedly be disastrous for the viewing figures), the teachings of the program when taken as a whole are almost wholly in line with the issues of attaining balance that Michael has referred to so often.

It is interesting to note that even the producer of the show recognises that Cesar, through his techniques and philosophies, has the ability to influence not only dogs but also their owners. She revels in the opportunities that they have to create such a positive impact and bring about change in other people's lives. She also recognises that this can come about just as a result of Cesar and the crew being there.

So what's actually going on with Cesar and this program?

Michael revealed that what makes Cesar so unusual is that he is an old soul who is performing a role that is distinctly within the province of young souls. He has perhaps unwittingly found fame and (presumably) fortune. This in itself is unusual for old souls since they do not seek the limelight because of the potential traps it holds for the ego. The power that wealth, status and public approbation can bring often tempts individuals away from fulfilling their soul contract of service. To be in the public eye and not give in to the seductive nature of its pleasures takes a rare individual, yet an examination of Cesar's life and activities reveals a wholehearted commitment to work for the highest good of all.

This is evident not only from the information and the way that it is presented but, by the account of the producer, also from the vibration of those involved in the program. This is a rare thing for media presentations. In fact, in the field of portraying creatures to the public, Cesar is one of a limited number (that would also include the Canadian environmentalist David Suzuki and the tragically fated Australian 'crocodile man'; Steve Urwin) of old souls.

Whether or not they are actually conscious of it, their soul purpose was in all cases the same: to reveal to the world the fundamentally synergistic nature of the relationship between humans and the natural world. Whilst approaching the issue from very different perspectives, each placed crucial information before the public at large and each has received special guidance in the way they do this. They have been (perhaps) unwitting channels for the angelic realms and the messages that they wish to deliver. Although they have undoubtedly agreed to this before incarnating, it should not be assumed that they are aware of it, since that knowledge in itself could prove a distraction.

It is interesting to watch Cesar if only because his inner light is so obviously visible. Every time we watch him, we wonder if he has undergone his own spiritual epiphany. In his manner and through all that he says and does, I cannot help but harbour a sneaking suspicion that he is a fully awakened individual. It is the fond wish of Sharon and me that one day we will get to meet him. In the dog world, he's our hero!

His teachings have also been massively enabling for us in managing our pack's energies since, quite apart from the general mayhem of having so many dogs, each presented their own unique challenges. These stem not from their individual personalities which are sweet and gentle, but from their interactions with one another. In this it is possible to observe parallels between the canine and the human world. At its most obvious this is simply of a case of not everybody likes everybody else, but they still all have to exist in the same space!

Regularly we are asked: "Do all of your dogs get on with one another" and the answer is a general "Yes" Most of the time they are tolerant and accepting but they are no better than humans. Conflicts sporadically break out and tensions can bubble. What is most interesting to note is the calming affects that being out in nature has on them all. Frustrations can be soothed away as a result of a walk in nature. Since the balance we chose within our lives (between our exposure to the natural world vs. that which we have to the man made world) is one of the issues that affects our ability to progress along our ascension pathway, I asked Michael about its general significance.

Balancing the natural vs. the man made world

We are of the natural world and yet we go to enormous lengths to shield ourselves from the environment and fabricate alternative experiences of living.

The affects of this are that we become out of balance with what is all around us. The more we attempt to 'tame' and the more we encroach upon the natural world, the more we damage ourselves. What is perceived as progress is often retrograde.

This does not imply that providing accommodation, places of work, shopping malls or facilities is bad. It is the degree to which we accept these as the totality of our reality that is unbalancing. The amount of time spent in one environment versus the other needs to be brought into balance.

To understand this, a parallel may be drawn:

The immensely popular Wii game, in its basic sport form, substitutes the reality of physically playing sport for sofa based game play. An individual can experience a clever facsimile of a sport that is not 'real'. The Wii version does not exercise the muscles of the body or, arguably, provide anything like the level of personal satisfaction that playing a sport can.

Thus it is with living: the environment in which many place themselves for the majority of their lifetimes is not the 'real' world. Only in this context it does not feed the soul.

If we cocoon ourselves in the reality which we create, there is a deeply held need, on a spiritual basis, that is not fulfilled. It is of great importance to us as individuals that we operate as a part of our broader environment and not the rarefied one that we create for the sake of convenience and comfort.

This is not to say that we should all go and live in the country or partake in the outdoors lifestyle. However, it will be confirmed by the majority dog owners that when they do something as simple as walk their pets in the outdoors, the experience has a profound effect upon their state of being.

This is because it helps, albeit in a very small way, to restore their level of balance.

Timba's arrival provided fresh challenges on a daily basis. As the months progressed it became a thing of extremes. On the one hand he would be highly affectionate and gentle with us, and then in an instant he would be exerting his very male energies to trying and dominate every single canine member of the pack. With some he would be subtle and cunning, (so Indy never seems to see him coming), whereas with others he will be overtly aggressive and domineering.

Eventually I needed to understand what was going on with him. This was not the balanced dog we were expecting. Michael was forthcoming:

Timba did not come into the world as the balanced version of Sage. He had the opportunity to ascend *if* he could achieve balance. Like every other being, to achieve that involved an on-going struggle for personal mastery. Furthermore, it was pointed out to us that Timba was not an avatar and that therefore he was affected by the energy line running through the house every bit as much as we humans.

Only the avatars were immune to the affects of the energy line since they effectively became a part of it. Within the non-avatars we could observe its impact in much the same way that we could upon ourselves because it accentuated the weaknesses in their personal balance: Pippa became needier; Emily became more independent; Molly became more frantic; Daisy became more moody. Only Ktuu seemed unaffected. But then as Michael had already explained, she had already come into balance and so had raised her vibration to be compatible with the energies of the line. She was totally on-track for ascension.

Timba's attempt to progress on his ascension pathway and ascend in this lifetime would be a very difficult one and a constant struggle, if only because of the energy line and its accentuation of his experiences. We had assumed that he was an old soul merely a step away from his goal and that coming to us would make things easy for him.

Quite to the contrary, it was now revealed that it would be very difficult for him and that the opportunity perceived by his higher self had been that it could make great leaps forward in learning and development as a result of dealing with adversity. He is not an old soul at all. The reason he has so much light energy is because he is actually a young soul. Sage's lifetime with all its torments and hardship was that of a baby soul. Timba, it transpired, was trying to get from being a young soul to ascension in a single lifetime.

As it turned out, Timba was not the only one who was being presented with challenges. It seemed that what we had agreed to do was also about to be stepped up several notches.

The Grid

That summer, as part of our Angels in Calgary initiative, Michael asked us to lead a number of guided hikes to his etheric retreat at Lake Louise.

We were to take parties to the spot and conduct channelling sessions in this unique and powerful location. The hike was just under twelve kilometres round trip but due to gradients and time spent there, it was a full day expedition. We had some wonderful experiences on our visits and it also provided us with ample opportunity for us to take those avatars capable of making the journey to a place where, Michael had advised us, they could become reacquainted with what they were.

How did the retreat affect the dogs?

The energies present at an etheric retreat may be experienced by all and it takes a seriously energy insensitive person not to get some form of reaction if they visit one of them. They may experience anything from tingling to indefinable strangeness or even full blown out-of-body sensations.

The affect upon dogs is probably even greater. The vibrations would be picked up through their noses and they would sense what was coming well in advance of their arrival. From an avatars perspective, the experience would be something close to an awakening in humans. It would have the effect of reconnecting them with their soul level DNA and produce a gentle reminder that they are not dogs, but something else in a dog's body.

Their response to the experience would alter greatly depending upon the maturity of the animal. A younger dog would most likely be more confused by the experience and although it would 'get it', the response would be more acute in an older animal.

We would begin the hikes in the parking lot by introducing our fellow hikers to whichever avatars were with us that day. It was a great opportunity to explain to participants something about the role they played, and although some were already aware of what avatars were, few had ever actually met one. It was interesting to note the transformation from the casual "Oh, they've brought a dog with them" type of response, to the reverence they then felt for them after they knew what they were. During the course of a day's hike, it would not be unusual for everyone to ask at some point: "Can I walk the dog for a while".

Perhaps the most interesting observation of the effect of the retreat's energies in action was when we took Cinnda with us. As I have already said, she was a shy and rather withdrawn animal who related to humans strictly on her own terms, which mostly meant not at all. During the hike she stayed on her leash with me and behaved impeccably. When we got to the channelling spot (an unfortunately uncomfortable place amidst rocks where it's difficult to find a place to rest) she immediately lay down and stretched herself out in what seemed to be a most painful position. As the channelling began she moved in close to me and nestled herself alongside me. And then when it was over, and the group had formed a circle to let the energies flow between us, she forced her way into the middle of the ring, curled up in a ball and just lay there, enjoying the energies. On the return journey she was a different dog. She became quite lively and sociable and I am pleased to report that she has been that way ever since.

It was on another hike a mere fortnight later with just two other people that instead of Michael, Archangel Gabriel visited during the channelling. He spoke of a purpose that we could undertake that would be of great benefit to the area, if we were willing. He didn't make it clear what that purpose was at that point but over the course of the next week he began to outline that he wanted us to plant what he called a crystal grid around a very large area of the Rockies.

We were to bury a quartz crystal at a point to the north of Lake Louise in a place called Twin Falls. When we got there we would be directed to the specific place where the crystal was to be buried and it was necessary for us to take one of the avatars with us. It would be the northern most point of a diamond shaped grid we were to plant. The crystals planted at the extremities would form anchoring points for the energies and for each planting the avatars (we would need to take a different one each time) would assist in the process. Indy was the designated dog of the north, Dougal the south, Kaiti the east and Briony the west. The north and south points required quartz and the east and west had to be amethyst. There was also to be a 'heart' where we would bury a piece of rose quartz and for this point we were to take Lara and Cinnda. The crystals had to be substantial pieces capable of amplifying the energies that would be run through them. Each of the four of us was to take it in turns to supply the crystals. Sharon and I would provide the north and south, Tanya the east and Garry the west. We would be directed to both the broad area and the specific points of burial as the need arose.

To be perfectly honest it all sounded a little bit crazy to me. This was something new to us (although we later came to understand that many other people had been directed to plant similar grids in places all over the planet). Ley lines, I thought I understood. The Light City I was just coming to terms with. But what was the point of burying crystals? It was with a great deal of hesitancy that I contacted our fellow hikers and explained what was being asked of us. To my surprise, they gladly accepted the task and a week later, we set off on our first 'planting' mission.

What was the purpose of planting the grid?

The purpose of the grid was something that was revealed to us over the course of the plantings. After each we would be visited by a being who would fill in a little more of the jigsaw puzzle of the information. Even now I won't pretend to fully understand it.

Like the energy line from the designated Light City, it was intended to assist in providing a network for the infusion of light energies into the earth to assist with planetary ascension.

The hike to Twin Falls was an experience that I shall never forget. We set off at 6.30am and arrived in the parking lot at the trailhead just after 9.00am. The sense of purpose and anticipation was immense and when we finally arrived at the falls after a breathtaking hike, Michael pointed

223

out the 'planting' spot. I had brought with me a large and beautiful piece of quartz that I had owned for a number of years. It was actually very sad to bury it. Michael explained the routine we were to go through, and having dug a suitably deep hole, cleansed, tuned, anointed and connected ourselves to the crystal, we put it back into the earth that it had originally sprung from.

The final part of this ceremony involved Indy and Michael explained that his avatar energies would be used to magnify and 'kick start' the energies that would flow through the grid. For his part, Indy seemed to know exactly what he was doing with no prompting and once we had replaced the earth to cover the crystal, he was very forthcoming with placing his great paws over the top of the hole.

Michael wanted me to channel for our little group and after I had delivered his message, he invited us to place our feet, one at a time, over the now filled hole. The experience was amazing. It was as if something was reaching up out of the ground and connecting with the sole of the foot. This he said, was the energy from the crystal that would eventually connect with all those within the grid that we would plant. Our task complete, we returned and arrived back at the car over ten hours and 22km after we had started.

Two weeks later we repeated the process planting the southern crystal, only this time with Dougal accompanying us in his official capacity as dog of the south and Molly along for the ride! Tanya was unable to do the hike for family reasons so it was just the three of us. I supplied another chunky piece of quartz, we replicated our first ceremonial planting almost exactly. Our avatar was every bit as compliant with his purpose as Indy had been. After we had finished, we once again had the experience of feeling the energy at our feet, but this time it ran towards the north and Michael explained that it was connecting with the northern crystal we had planted a fortnight before. I wasn't sure how the dogs were responding to the energies, but they didn't seem to mind and I guessed that the very long walks were adequate compensation for anything.

Two weeks after that, we started out for the eastern point only this time we were missing Garry who was ill. Also that day Kaiti was a little out of sorts, so we left her behind and took Indy again as a stand-in. For the first time, the weather was bad and we began in heavy rain, shrouded by a grey and bleak sky. It was not an auspicious beginning but we pressed on regardless. A sign on the trailhead warned that the area we were meant to go to was closed due to grizzly bear activity, a not uncommon thing in the Rockies. However, Michael said that we could plant the crystal as near to the spot as possible, so we set off.

Several hours later we stopped for lunch and Tanya decided that this was as good a spot as any to plant the crystal, despite the fact that Michael was telling me it was the wrong place. We had lunch and whilst we were eating, Tanya got out her piece of amethyst. Immediately, I felt a sickening feeling in my stomach. It was a beautiful piece of very high grade crystal, but it was tiny. I bit my tongue and said nothing and we continued with lunch.

Meanwhile Tanya wandered off and when she returned some while later she announced that she had planted the crystal. Sharon and I were struck dumb. We had not performed any aspect of the planting ceremony that Michael had directed us to perform and the avatar (even though it was technically the wrong one), had not been there to energise the crystal. Gently we explained what the problem was and fortunately, Tanya allowed us to dig it up again. As it turned out, she had simply covered it with moss. We went through the ceremony and then returned to our lunch spot a few yards away to hear what Michael had to say to us.

When I'd finished channelling and returned to my body, Sharon was looking at me uneasily. Michael had expressed his gratitude for our work as before, but had seemed a little nonplussed in his expression. Tanya was positively disenchanted as this was 'her' planting. But Sharon's increasingly concerned look had nothing to do with disappointment. Apparently I had now gone grey and my cheeks looked as if they had been hollowed out. Scarily, when I stood up I was very unsteady and my trousers were (somewhat miraculously) too big for me. In fifteen minutes I had lost at least two inches off my waistline!

Stunned, I asked Michael what was happening. His reply was brief and to the point. The crystal was not big enough to hold the energies that were required to run through it. It could only serve as a temporary anchoring point as it would not be able to properly connect with the other points. He showed me an image of the line running between the north and south points and then their connections to this eastern crystal. At this point the energies slowed and became very fine in their flow. It needed to be replaced as soon as possible. We had also brought the wrong avatar so in order to compensate for this the initiating energies had been run through me! However, if I told Tanya these truths, I should be aware that she would no longer participate in our hikes!

I'm not one to avoid the truth so I explained it as sensitively as I could. Tanya took it very well and we agreed that we would mark the spot of the planting and return to replace the crystal when we had one of a more suitable size. She only had one concern: Whilst she could not deny the physical impact upon me, if the energies that had been run through me were healing in nature and for the highest good of the planet, how come I was now a walking wreck? Why was I having difficulty with my movement, relying totally upon my walking stick and even speaking very slowly? Surely that wasn't right?

The answer was instantaneous: The energies had been intended for the earth and not for a human being. Whilst I could tolerate them because I was being protected, their power was not compatible with my physical structure. As they had passed through me, they had washed all my energy away with them. The hollowed cheeks and startling weight loss were physical symptoms of the affect, as was the greying of my skin. Whilst I would certainly recover, it would take several hours.

The walk home was fraught by failing limbs and falling trousers. I had noted with glee whenever we were doing these hikes that I felt positively supercharged. I finished the hikes feeling every bit as good as I had at the start, and although aching limbs always set in later, while I was out there I was unstoppable. Now I was a wreck and the walk back was one of the hardest physical experiences of my life. Normally I was way out in front but during our slow progress back to the parking lot I lagged behind and was unable to keep up.

By the time we arrived back at the car I had begun to feel better, but the experience had certainly taken its toll. It was not until two days later that I felt like myself again. When we dropped Tanya off, all seemed to be fine, but I told Sharon about Michael's warning on the way home and we debated whether or not she would actually withdraw.

Of course the discussion was futile. Just as Michael had forewarned, Tanya wrote an email to us next week saying that she did not believe that her crystal was too small and that clearly I was hearing wrong information. Consequently she no longer wished to participate in our hikes. She absolutely did not accept that the crystal needed to be replaced. However, we could have it as her contribution to the initiative.

The following weekend we repeated the hike. This time the sunshine was glorious, Garry was with us and so was Kaiti. We almost flew the first part of the hike, dug up the crystal from its moss covered resting place, walked considerably further and closer to the intended resting place (even entering the forbidden grizzly bear area). We found a first class place for our ceremony. We buried a huge amethyst bed with another slightly smaller one on top and crowned it with Tanya's crystal. It made a beautiful pyramid and we felt the energy flow with no physical problems for me. Kaiti, awkward as ever, refused to co-operate with the planting. Clearly her knowledge of her purpose had not included this! Nevertheless, we succeeded in getting the energy to run through her and our task was complete. We even had great pictures of a remarkable day. The difference in experience was striking. Michael pointed out that it was merely an example of how things could be if things were allowed to happen as they were meant to!

Two weeks later we did the western hike with Briony and she was perfect. A week after that we set out for the heart with a huge piece of heart shaped rose quartz and the two Huskies. The planting ceremony went without a hitch and Lara was co-operative. Cinnda went and lay down on the hole and stayed there as I did the after-planting channelling. No less than six angels and Masters came through with a remarkable if complex explanation of our purpose. Even more amazingly, they told us that we had now created an energy vortex in this place. I was just the slightest bit hesitant in my acceptance of this but after a few minutes we were all shocked to see a wave of energy flowing

227

around us in a broadly arcing circle. At first I thought it was a heat haze until we realised that it was October and that the temperatures were only just above zero degrees centigrade.

Please can you find me an avatar?

At twelve dogs, enough is enough! We knew that at some point we would have to let the Lara avatar have puppies, but in the meantime, there was no need for any more dogs. The energy line was doing its thing without any issues and all we had to do was be effective in helping the avatars manage their energies.

We have many friends who know all about our pack and their origins. We tend to attract those who either share our beliefs or accept them and therefore for them it goes without question that they are avatars. It is also the case that we know many who are able to perceive their energies would gladly welcome an avatar into their own homes.

So it came as no surprise that we were asked by our good friends Angie and Diego if we could track down an avatar for them and their family. They had two daughters, Valeria and Natalia, both of whom were pressuring their parents to get them a dog and Angie and Diego were by no means reluctant. Usually my response to this would be to advise that parents should NEVER get a dog because a child wants one. Too often they are temporary sources of amusement that children get bored with and their care falls to uninterested adults. It is a recipe for pain if ever there was one and I would normally politely disavow my ability to assist. However, I knew both of their daughters quite well and I believed that they understood at an innate spiritual level the benefits to having a synergistic relationship with an animal. Michael confirmed this and therefore I did not give my customary response.

Bearing in mind that avatars come with a specific purpose, it is not actually possible to get one unless there is a pre-existing intention that they be with you. However, anybody can potentially get a 'second-hand' one. By this I mean one that has fulfilled its purpose and been moved on, as was the case with Cinnda. As I have already stated that only .0003% of all dogs are avatars, this may appear to be like looking for a needle in a haystack; but with angelic guidance, it is by no means an impossible task. So I agreed to the request.

Fortunately, the family in question wanted a Husky and this made things a lot easier, since all I then had to do was look at Husky rescue sites.

Why did wanting a Husky make things easier?

In DNA terms, a Husky is the closest fully domesticated dog to a wolf that exists today. Therefore it is a very pure representation of the life from which it came. Because of this, the light that the avatar possesses and emits is able to pass through the creature's structure with ease and its purpose of bringing light and healing energies may be achieved with a relative lack of difficulty. A Husky is therefore the obvious choice of body for an avatar.

Of course many individuals would not wish to own a Husky or consider having one as a pet. Under these circumstances the avatar must incarnate within another breed dog and it is certainly not the case that all avatars are Huskies.

However, on balance there are more avatars which are Huskies because there are those who choose to get a dog which unbeknownst to them it will be coming as an avatar. Often they will be 'influenced' to get a Husky.

The brief they gave was quite specific: they wanted a male puppy that was white with blue eyes. I had to explain that finding an avatar to order is pretty much an impossibility.

Nevertheless, I began to search for one. Initially I trawled the sites from all across Canada and whilst finding Huskies in need of rescue was no issue whatsoever, on this occasion I found no avatars. (Don't forget that for every three thousand that I viewed, only one was likely to be an avatar.) So I moved on to the US sites and with a wider pool, greater chances emerged. Within a few hours I had tracked an avatar in Colorado.

How did I track down the avatar?

Finding dog recue sites on the internet is as easy as falling off a log. At any one time there are tens of thousands of homeless creatures seeking new homes and hundreds of websites for learning about them. For many types of dogs there are breed specific rescue centres or individuals who specialise in rehoming just that breed.

I scan the pictures very rapidly and as they flick by, I get a sense from looking at them as to whether or not they are these precious beings. It is an almost magnetic sense of attraction that comes from somewhere deep within me. It begins as a tingling sensation and a need to stop and look. If I think it is one, I always ask for confirmation because I want to be 100% sure, and I don't always get it right. A lot of dogs that may look angelic are not avatars and appearances can be very deceptive.

The physical sensation is as a result of an energetic connection being established with the avatar. Once begun this link is very hard for me to break. The more I look at them, the stronger the connection becomes until it is something that they may also sense if they are aware.

On the one hand, it enables me to find and recognise them. On the other, it is a potential source of pain to them: An 'awakened' avatar will have a higher level of sentience than a normal dog; it is acutely aware of the precarious nature of its homelessness and seeks to return to an environment where it could extend its third dimensional experience and more freely 'shine its light'. The connection that enables me to locate them is returned to them as a source of hope which may then be unfulfilled, causing more heartache for them.

It is difficult for me to look at any dog that has found itself in a shelter and not feel tremendous sadness and pity.

When I find an avatar, I feel an almost insurmountable need to help them. One day I will found an avatar rescue that offers sanctuary for those angelic beings that have fulfilled their purpose and been cast aside.

It was an absolutely gorgeous dog and very obviously an avatar from my perspective. The problem was that it was a black and white female, four years old with brown eyes called Mookie! It couldn't have been further from their stated requirements. So I carried on looking and shortly thereafter, came across another avatar in Montana. However, this match was even worse: A thirteen year old male with a red and white coat and hazel eyes called Joe.

Whilst I was checking out the accuracy of my recognition Michael revealed that there was another avatar at this rescue centre, but it was not depicted. So I carried on looking and on yet another site I found another, but this one was a twelve year old blind Malamute. I could quite easily imagine the learning she had elected to bring to her owner, as well as that which the avatar might have wished for itself, though this did not prevent me from finding her situation heartbreaking. Who would want a twelve year old blind dog?

That night I sent pictures of Mookie and Joe to our friends but immediately after I had done so, Michael pointed out that the purpose in finding Joe was that we might like to consider having him ourselves! "Why, when we have already agreed to have the puppies, do we need another avatar?" I asked in exasperation. The explanation was clear but a little disheartening:

Why did we need another avatar?

In areas where are there are designated light cities, there is also an attraction for negative, denser or darker energies that have the effect of countering the positives of the light energies.

In response to the growing power of the Light City, the city most local to our home was experiencing considerable 'darkness', which was manifesting itself principally through a rise in violent crime.

This effect had been anticipated. The puppies were a way to combat that effect because each and every avatar amplified the positive effects of the energy line in their capacity as 'step up transformer'. Their only purpose in coming to us would be to perform this role and had we not lived there, we would never have found ourselves in the position of receiving them.

However, the puppies were not with us yet and the undesirable effects of the negative energies to the east were growing stronger; therefore any additional avatars that we could take could provide useful assistance.

Avatars in rescue had already performed their initial service and attempted to perform the role that was predestined for them. They still had a great deal of value on the earthly planes in assisting as conduits for healing energies around the line.

So after getting the go ahead from Sharon, (who by now had adopted a somewhat resigned approach to the knowledge that all this was happening for the highest good) I contacted the rescue shelter. I also contacted the rescue with the blind Malamute to ask if they thought that she could cope with living amongst a large pack of dogs. I thought it was a long shot, but worth asking nonetheless.

The next day I heard back from Helena, the lady who ran Joe's rescue shelter and began the now familiar process of being vetted. I also heard from the blind Malamute's shelter but they confirmed that she would not be able to cope with the confusion that would result from so many other dogs being around her. However, it was good to be in communication because it left me with a much stronger sense that at the very least, this particular avatar was being well loved and cared for, although I should not have been surprised.

Why shouldn't I have been surprised?

I have not yet come across anybody involved in animal rescue who I do not consider to be some form of saint. They care passionately about the creatures they are protecting and almost put their own needs in second place to those of the animals. Animal welfare can be a very expensive

233

thing with the massive costs of providing veterinary care, food and accommodation. Yet they do it without question.

What many don't realise is that it is a spiritual calling to do this. Their attraction to the animals is no accident and they are experiencing a lifetime of animal synergy. In some respects it is no different from those who are in the medical profession except that it goes beyond this calling. To reach out to offer support to another species that is suffering is not 'second nature' and as such it represents a different level of comprehension of the world around us.

Many in the medical profession are midterm souls. The majority of those involved in both veterinary care and animal rescue are older souls whose depth of comprehension of all that is, at a subconscious level, is greater. Ironically they may not realise it themselves.

That night we were due to see Angie and Diego for dinner which is always a delightful experience. But as soon as we met them I was horrified when they told us how much they had fallen in love with Joe, despite the fact that he did not match with their profile of their ideal avatar! They had shown their daughters pictures of him and they all thought he was wonderful.

I then had the hideously embarrassing experience of having to explain that I had 'jumped the gun' and that Michael himself had told *me* to get Joe. They accepted this with good grace but it still felt a bit like I was fobbing them off with an excuse that was geared to satisfy my own needs. Michael had been quite clear that Mookie could be a good dog for them, and I was grateful that they were also attracted to her.

Setting up the collection of Joe was hindered firstly by the imminence of Christmas, but also by the bad weather that both Montana and Alberta were experiencing. So after one postponement, we made plans to collect Joe at a date that would be five weeks after our initial contact.

In the meantime, we were surprised to receive an email from the lady with the blind Malamute asking if we would consider taking a dog that was currently in North Dakota. It was another elderly white Malamute named Kira and Michael assured us that this too was an avatar. The woman had been guided to point it out to us since it was not at a shelter whose site that I had come across, being Malamute rather than Husky rescue (although they are often combined). Again, after receiving Sharon's consent, I began the vetting process. We calculated that if we combined Joe's collection in Montana with Kira's in North Dakota, then we could do a three day round trip to get them both.

Two days before we were due to collect Joe, despite several emails we had still not heard from the Malamute people. Then late that evening we received a message saying that they did not feel that we would be the right home for Kira. We were quite disappointed but also frustrated since an Archangel seemed to think that we would be! Michael reminded us that the intervention of free will could prevent that which was for the highest good from happening although he too felt that their refusal was unfortunate.

<u>Wouldn't the avatars be bringing benefit wherever they were?</u>

In what I describe here there is almost an implication that these avatars would automatically be better off with us. I do not mean to suggest this. As I have already said, rescuers provide lots of loving care for their charges.

Principal behind my reasoning is the fact Archangel Michael had led us to these dogs and on that basis alone, I consider that Kira *should* have been with us.

One of the unique features of us proving a home for avatars is their ability to enhance the energy line and from this perspective, being members of our household allows them to serve the highest good of all.

In the meantime Angie and Diego had been told by the Colorado rescue that they couldn't have Mookie because they lived too far away, so things were not going too well.

It meant that three avatars that I knew of were not finding their way out of rescue centres.

Special needs: Joe and Saffy's tale

Less than twenty four hours before we were due to begin our journey to Montana we received a telephone message and an email from Helena asking if we might be able to provide assistance with a dog named Saffy. She was deaf and had liver disease. She had been with her owner for thirteen years but had apparently snapped at a grandchild and therefore was going to be 'moved on'. The shelter, in an effort to exert some emotional leverage upon these people told them that nobody would take a dog at that age and in that condition, so if they really couldn't keep a loyal pet that had been with them for so long, it would be kinder to have her put to sleep. In response, they actually decided that this was a good option. In the meantime the shelter desperately searched for someone who would help. Although she wasn't an avatar, Michael again referred to this as an 'act of kindness' and we agreed, even though it meant extending our journey by hundreds of kilometres.

So early on Friday we set out on the eight hour drive to the hotel where we would stay overnight before collecting Joe and Saffy the next day. Another early start was followed by a three hour drive through heavy snow to the shelter that housed over sixty dogs. Joe was waiting for us in the front yard, a big woolly bear of a dog with a thick ginger and white coat and deep amber coloured eyes. He was friendly but a little guarded and clearly quite bonded to Helena. He followed us into her house and was overcome by the excitement of this unexpected pleasure. As we chatted he put his nose in everything and seemed delighted to have the temporary privilege of being an indoor dog.

After a while Helena offered to show us round and it was a remarkable experience walking around in the falling snow and meeting so many wonderful creatures. We were aghast that their owners could have abandoned them in the way that they had. Helena explained that because of the world financial crisis and the credit squeeze, many more dogs than usual were being 'dumped' in shelters. I wasn't just listening to her though: along the way I learned that there were not one but three other avatars at this place. Helena positively shone with light and I wondered if she herself had some angelic connection.

When we had done the tour she explained that Joe and his brother had been owned by a man who, in the early years of their lives, had looked after them well. In later years he had become an alcoholic and had descended into the depths of his drinking habit. Gradually he began to forget to feed the dogs and as he was in a constant state of alcoholic stupor, they became progressively more neglected.

It was unclear how long it took him to get to this stage or how long the dogs suffered this hardship. What was known was that Joe's brother eventually died of starvation. The smell alerted the neighbours who called the police. His rotting corpse, was found next to Joe who was barely alive. They had been chained up together, possibly for years. At some point Joe had been crudely 'debarked'.

A vet determined that he could survive and might once have been a nice dog, so he remained in a dog pound for six months before economics set his execution date. At the eleventh hour he was grasped from the jaws of death by the lady who ran the rescue and he came to live with her. It took another full year before he returned to health, but still was unable to walk properly as he suffered great weakness in his hind quarters, probably as a result of being beaten. Finally she figured that he might benefit from a 'forever' home where he would receive lots of loving attention. She advertised him on the rescue website. Nobody seemed to want a thirteen year old deaf dog with thyroid issues until Michael said we might like to go and get him. But we didn't tell Helena this part.

You might think that a dog that has gone through such horrific experiences might be terrified of humans. At the very least it might be reasonable to bear a grudge or have some shyness. Perhaps because he is an avatar Joe greeted us as friends and with affection. All he seemed to desire was a little company and occasional attention. I asked Michael what his purpose had been and it was very saddening to learn that he had not met with the success that had been hoped for. It was a consolation for us to know that at least the avatar could go on to achieve another purpose and be of benefit elsewhere.

What was Joe's original purpose?

The owner's life had reached a personal nadir with the breakup of his marriage. He was a midterm soul (in the later stages), having the need to break free of his ego's control over himself. It was always intended that this experience be one of his worst signposts; but at the point of this painful event happening, he would reach a crossroads. He could look outside of himself for help, or within.

The marriage breakdown cost him his friends and ultimately his job. He found himself on welfare left with the unwanted residue of his former life: two stupidly devoted and trusting dogs. They were what he could have reached out to. They loved him unconditionally and without judgement. They could have restored his need for belonging and acceptance and provided him with purpose and reason. Tragically for them, he never reached out. He simply abandoned them in his self absorption.

I wondered why this purpose required an avatar. Any dog could have provided this devotion. But it was a little more complex than that:

His spiralling response was always a danger to the dogs. It was his choice to try and break free of it. If he managed it, the experience was to form an awakening for him. It required the creature that went through the ghastly experience to come away from it with complete and unearthly forgiveness; and the unique avatar energies within Joe would not only have provided this, they would also have provoked his awakening.

There would have come a point when the owner could have stared into those big amber eyes and seen something other than a dog staring back. In a flash of soul recognition that would have been felt at the level of his soul's DNA, he would have remembered that there was something else beyond his own self destructive ego. It would have been an epiphany of the first order that would have passed between them in miraculous spark of knowing.

But he never looked.

When we came to leave we loaded Joe into the back of our SUV but Helena was unable to come and say goodbye to the dog she had cared for so much.

We continued our journey east for another three hours. In mid afternoon we arrived and drove straight to the rescue centre. There we were met by one of the workers who held a leash attached to a walking skeleton. Looking at her, it was a miracle that she was alive and it seemed that the version of what had befallen her had been understated to say the least.

The rescue worker was barely able to contain her anger as she relayed the story of the heartless manner in which the owners had felt able to rid themselves of their dog as if she were a disposable item. Huskies can easily live to fifteen or older if well looked after. This dog should have had more years left in her. They seemed to feel no sense of responsibility despite her having shared thirteen years of their lives. The liver disease could account for some of the thinness but the concentration camp victim like appearance of this dog also seemed to imply massive under feeding.

We put Saffy on the back seat with a too big dog seatbelt designed for a Husky that was not totally emaciated and began our journey home. Our new travelling companions seemed in very good spirits. They were totally unphased by the experience and Saffy seemed to think that it was great! She was lively and excited and really enjoyed standing with her head between our seats, looking at the road ahead. How much she could actually see was a moot point, but that didn't really matter!

It took several hours to dawn on me that both dogs were deaf and from that point onward, our journey was characterised by very loud music intended to keep sleep at bay. We had estimated that we could probably make it no further than a town just north of the Canadian border before fatigue set in, and sure enough, by the time we reached it I had been driving for fourteen hours of that day and I was exhausted.

At 11.30pm we checked into our dog friendly hotel and Joe and Saffy decided that it was playtime. For the next two hours they ran up and down the small room like a couple of naughty puppies. In desperation I took them for a brief walk at 1.30am when the thermometer read minus 25C outside. I finally got to sleep sometime after 2.00am but at 3.15am Joe decided that he wanted to out again. After half an hour of walking (now at minus 27C) we returned to the hotel and after what seemed like minutes of fitful sleep they woke us again at 4.30am.

We decided to give up and go home. Sleep deprivation and a road devoid of wake-me-up stimuli forced us to pull into a car park at one of the very few towns on our route. It was 6.30am. After half an hour we woke up reasonably refreshed. We struggled on, eventually finding a coffee shop and despite being served appallingly weak black liquid, we managed to get home at around 10.30am.

Upon our arrival, we went through the usual meet and greet procedures, letting each dog from the household encounter their new pack mates individually. It all went well apart from Indy taking an instant dislike to Joe. In response Joe was utterly oblivious to his dominant posturing. It was a good reminder that avatars do not behave like we might expect angels to!

Saffy was very excited to become part of a pack but she was so old and frail that she was unable to participate in their most lively activities. She was enrapt by the amount of land to wander and stayed outside for a long time just exploring the space. Joe quickly decided that it was much more interesting inside and within minutes, just as Cinnda had done before him, he established himself as a 'house Husky'. It took just a few hours longer for Saffy to decide that she was prepared to live in our house too.

After the initial caution borne from arriving in a totally new and alien environment, they were 'old hands' within a week. The hindquarters of both dogs proved to be very weak and they had great difficulty with stairs so they both now sleep on the ground floor. A magnetic collar went a long way to solving Joe's stiffness but Saffy's unsteadiness proved to be more due to her advanced age and general weakness.

She also seemed to be suffering from senile dementia and incontinence. If she went outside, she could not find her way back to the house and a search and rescue party would have to be sent out. We had to get a reflective collar for her so that in the dark we could shine a torch and spot her otherwise invisible form. Following her initial euphoria at being amongst the pack, she became quite withdrawn and confused. She was unresponsive to us, and showed very little interest in human contact. It looked like she was going downhill and we began to fear that her stay with us would be short lived.

After a couple of weeks, there was a very unfortunate incident where Saffy 'pancaked'. Her legs were completely splayed out as if she was doing the four-legged splits and she was completely unable to move. Sharon and Jenny rushed to assist her as she was in the midst of other dogs that might not be sympathetic to her plight. In her obvious terror, Saffy lashed out and bit both of them and in response to seeing his beloved Jenny attacked by another creature, Indy moved in for the kill. It was only Sharon yelling loudly that prevented a tragic set of consequences coming into being and the situation was resolved with only human bloodshed.

Afterwards Saffy went into some form of toxic shock. The terrifying experience was clearly killing her and that night we prepared ourselves for the worst. Both Sharon and Jenny (who is also a powerful energy healer) set to work on her pathetic little body and the effects were astounding. Not only did she recover, she also seemed to get younger and her senility disappeared!

Within days we found ourselves with a quite active and very happy dog that runs around quite happily with the rest of the dogs and has apparently also started to de-age. She is becoming increasingly more affectionate and although her weight is still woefully inadequate, we are now hopeful that she might be with us for a lot longer than her previous owners might have anticipated.

Privately, what I am also delighted about is the fact that Sharon and Jenny took being bitten as if it were of no consequence. Although Jenny's wound was superficial and quickly recovered, Sharon has been left with a scar on her forearm but she has never even mentioned it and treats Saffy with the same loving attentions as she does any of the other dogs.

Joe quickly established himself as a major character. At first he was quite aloof and guarded but very quickly began to greet us in the mornings with a little skipping act he developed that is highly comical. Whilst this has a lot to do with his first great love, food, he also is full of joy when we return from shopping or any slightly prolonged absence. He exudes goodwill and love of everybody and he is immensely affectionate. The contrast between both him (and Timba) and other male Huskies that we have encountered is quite stark. He is playful and giving and simply adorable.

His one Achilles heel is definitely his attitude towards food. Joe had been used to kibble when he was in the rescue center. Before that we think it is likely that he scavenged waste bins or got nothing. He thinks nothing of attacking the bins in our house and will quite happily take whatever food is within reach and his is quite indiscriminate in his choice of foods. Recently he ate a loaf and a half of bread, a zucchini, a packet of pine nuts and bit into the wrapper of a Mars bar. Fortunately we caught that one before he could actually eat any! Nothing is safe and those weak back legs are now strong enough to stand up on and reach all of the kitchen work surfaces. None of this makes him any the less adorable and we are very grateful that he has come to be with us.

After we'd had them for a few weeks, Angie, Diego and the girls came to spend the day with us. They adored Joe who they were now meeting for the first time. I felt a little guilty, but in not so many words, Michael told me to get over it: What had happened was for the highest good of all.

An energy spike: The puppies

The highest good of all is not always in line with personal expectations of what should come to pass, particularly when expectations are based on false assumptions. You may have realised that throughout the story we have been very good at these! And so it was with Lara's puppies.

Shortly after her season finished, I decided to check conventional wisdom on whether or not Timba could possibly father puppies at a mere six months old. Different internet sites gave different versions of the facts but although the answer was not exactly conclusive, there seemed to be a fair chance that he could.

Naturally we asked Michael whether or not we would become 'grandparents' and he found the question quite amusing. He reiterated that the arrival of the puppies was a very important thing for the energy line and told us to "wait and see". Sharon took this as a firm "Yes".

From that point onwards there were two strands of thought in the house. Sharon's that accepted that Lara was pregnant and mine that was in denial that any puppies would be coming our way. In part I felt this way because Lara simply didn't look pregnant; in part it was because I never believed that it would happen so soon. Whilst we had accepted that it was important to allow her to have them and that it was pretty much an inevitability, I just couldn't envisage that it would happen so soon. After all, both dogs were just babies!

Denial did not prevent speculation and we had many debates about how many puppies there would be. Sharon was convinced (or at least she was desperately hoping) that there would only be two. As you may recall, Michael had already said that "at least three of them would be avatars" so I thought that a minimum of three was a very safe bet; whereas Susan, Buddy's owner, was adamant that there would be four. Huskies are known for having small litters so any of us could potentially be right. We began to think of names but this produced conflicts as we were trying to find thematically compatible names and Sharon would think of duo's while I would suggest trio's. Susan spent some time and effort coming up with a series of well thought out individual names that were great, but had no theme. So by the time they were born, no mutually acceptable names had been arrived at.

With what was to prove just over two weeks to go, Lara became noticeably 'fat' so finally conceding that something was indeed happening, I set about constructing a whelping box. Lara seemed to know instinctively what this was and when I put her in it, she was quite relaxed. The other dogs also seemed to know that this was her 'den' and stayed well clear of it, despite its prominent position in front of the basement fireplace, usually immensely popular for its warmth. I spent time researching what would happen during the birth on the internet. The last time I had been present at the birth of an animal was when a friend's father who was a vet took us on his rounds when I was six. I had watched him deliver a calf with complete disinterest. It was not nearly as exciting as playing on the hay bales in the barn where the cow gave birth. Now, I eagerly anticipated what would happen and found the whole process enthralling.

However, when the puppies started to arrive, the first one seemed to miraculously appear in the well of a pedestal desk, the most cave-like spot in the house. I was a little bit disappointed that she did not use the whelping box I had so loving constructed, but even more so that I didn't even see it happen; it was so quick and Lara did a very good job of hiding what was going on. I had feared that as she was such a young mother she would have trouble with the births or perhaps not know what to do.

She was to prove me utterly wrong and I found it awesome that her responses to what was happening were text book illustrations of what a dog was supposed to do upon delivering puppies. After a few minutes, Lara let me take her first daughter and move it to the whelping box so that it would be in the warmest place.

Since none of this had begun until after midnight, Sharon had already retired to bed. The first birth happened too quickly to call her, but now I woke her up to see her 'grandchild'. We watched as Lara spent the next half hour washing her new baby before leaping out of the box and pacing madly in what I now recognised as the build up to another birth.

The second daughter was delivered on the floor of the family room, but the puppy came out backwards and got stuck around the neck. Lara was clearly distressed by this and I felt quite privileged that she allowed me to help pull it out. Immediately she went to work cleaning it up and after a while this one was moved to the whelping box too. Lara fussed over the puppies while I took pictures of the newborns. There was no sign that anything else would happen so Sharon happily concluded that she had been right about the number being born and returned to bed.

If an Archangel has told you something, the chances of it being wrong are very slim, so it came as no surprise to me that two and half hours later, another puppy began to emerge as if by magic and with seemingly no effort on Lara's part. However, this one was even more stuck than the second and I found myself playing midwife yet again. Not only this, its birth sack seemed to be particularly tough and Lara was unable to penetrate it with her teeth. It is quite something to rip open the membrane and allow a puppy to take its first breath. I was in awe of the experience and once I had produced an opening Lara quickly finished the rest.

Can angels tell you anything that is wrong?

Nothing that we have ever had revealed to us has been wrong and as has already been mentioned, they certainly cannot lie to you. In some instances there is potential for outcomes to be affected by freedom of choice, but if this is the case, it is made clear to us at the time.

In a matter like this we should have just listened.

This time I had my camera ready straight away and I was able to photograph this third baby girl within thirty seconds of it being cleared of the membrane by the mother.

Lara was getting thirsty by this time so I rushed upstairs to freshen her bowl. As I was doing so, I called triumphantly up to Sharon that there were now three! But by the time I got downstairs I was wrong too as a forth puppy was now emerging. This one also required help and after it had been cleaned, Lara finally allowed the puppies to feed. I now remembered reading that this would only happen when all of the puppies had been born. The last born was a boy and I was delighted when Michael confirmed that they were *all* avatars.

I slept the rest of that night (and all of my nights for the next two weeks) on the floor next to the box. In the morning the children stopped by on their way to school to see the puppies and left with the smile that only puppies seem to engender. "That's a good way to begin the day" said Jenny.

It so happened that at the time of the births our television was in the repair shop, a fact that had previously been a cause for great distress for Tristan. In the weeks that followed the puppies were to prove a great compensation and I was surprised that even when the puppies were at their youngest and effectively did nothing, both children would sit and watch them for hours on end. "It's better than TV" said Jenny, and we all had to agree.

Within twenty four hours of their birth, we had agreed upon names. Quite by accident we discovered that Lara was the Russian word for light. We hadn't known it when we named her and reflected that it was a particularly apt name for an avatar. So we looked up other words for light and as a consequence the four puppies were named, in order of their birth: Inara (shining light); Aura (light filled); Zoe (life filled with light) and Idaho (the Sioux word for 'light upon the mountains'). It all seemed very appropriate to us.

Around thirty six hours after their birth we took them to see the vet just for a check up. She was surprised by how lively and inquisitive they were. I didn't tell her that it was because they were all angels.

Interest in the puppies amongst our friends was great. We received several enquiries about their potential adoption and disappointed many that we simply weren't letting any of them go. Because they are avatars their attraction was great. Many who had never owned a dog before wanted one 'just because'. However, Michael made it very clear that they were to serve their purpose in this place and that was why we had them in the first place. The Lara avatar's desire to have puppies was

248

secondary to the need to bring in their additional energies to reinforce the current coursing through the energy line. Their sustained presence (and by this he meant full lifetimes, as opposed to lesser ones of the older avatars we have) was vital for the consistency of the flow.

The effect of the puppies upon the energy line was instantaneous and massive. It was as if they provided an energy surge which was not so much of a 'spike' as an ongoing raising of the current. All of the disruptions that we had just begun to get used to now underwent a huge magnification and once again we had to go through the concomitant trials and tribulations. We were not the only ones to experience the imbalance it created: About eleven kilometres up the line is a school a few hundred metres off the west of its path. It had always been a troubled place due to its proximity, but now things started to get really bad. Within three weeks, three teachers and the principal had resigned.

"Everything that comes to pass is for the highest good of all" Michael reminded me.

Making sense of a dog's life

The purpose of all things is to progress along their ascension pathway, and dogs are no different. The things that happen to them across the course of their lives all contribute to that which they had intended for themselves. A particular owner may receive great benefit from a lifetime of experience with a pet, but in return, the pet receives benefit from them. The lifetimes are synergistic.

Depending upon their soul level a dog may have made specific agreements with other beings. This may be to play a part in their learning, perhaps in their awakening (as with Buddy and Susan) and certainly with their general life experience. The seeming barriers between species have no meaning when we consider that we are all beings of light. No life is meaningless and each and every being has its purpose. It is unfortunate that from our limited perspective we cannot necessarily see what it is.

I once received an email from a distraught lady called Jean who was involved in animal rescue. In particular she dealt with the rehabilitation of dogs that would otherwise be euthanized and she made her home open to pets that had been subjected to the worst kind of abuse and torture. Emotionally damaged dogs and those with the severe issue were all welcomed and if she could not cope herself, she was brilliant at networking to find secure homes for these outcasts.

She had been contacted by the daughter of a lady who owned a handicapped dog called Kellie, a six year old Border Collie who could only move about with the aid of a dog wheelchair since she had no use of her rear legs. In all respects Kellie was still a very 'alive' dog. She was very loving and active despite her wheelchair bound status and was considered an excellent candidate for service in pet-assisted therapy. Sadly the lady was very elderly and could no longer look after the dog. Her daughter was seeking help in finding the dog a new home so without any hesitation Jean committed to find her a safe haven. In the meantime Kellie was handed over to a 'caregiver' who professed great love for the dog and she in turn allowed a young boy who was interested in working with dogs to enrol Kellie in a Pets As Therapy

251

program. The dog was the absolute star of the class, highly responsive to the learning and clearly relishing her usefulness. Both the animal and the boy clearly found the experience richly rewarding and bond formed between them.

Over a month before the training program was due to end, Jean received an email from the daughter. Apparently she had been contacted by the caregiver who confessed to not having been totally honest with her about Kellie. She explained that although she liked her and had promised to look after her until the P.A.T. program finished (giving Jean time to find her a home) she now believed that she should be 'put down' immediately. She claimed that she had been unaware of how much time she would have to devote to Kellie and she didn't think that it was right to keep a dog with her disability alive although she admitted that Kellie herself was perfectly happy.

The daughter herself found the situation unfair because she did not have time to cope and couldn't bring her back home since she believed that it would upset both the dog and her mother. She too believed that this pet could have a good life with the right owner but expressed concern that she would be rejected repeatedly as others would not understand her disabilities and the amount of time she required. Reluctantly therefore, she concurred with the caregiver.

Jean knew exactly what the needs were for this poor creature and more besides so she left telephone messages for the daughter imploring her to just let her take Kellie. Jean herself would assume all of the burden and anyone else involved would be free of responsibility. When these went unanswered, she tried to contact her through the local vet's office. This failed too, so she sent emails. In them she promised to provide a forever, loving home for Kellie. She pointed out her 24/7 availability for the dogs, her vast experience in dealing with the problems the dog had, her expertise in massage therapy that would support her physical hardships and even the fact that she was due to get a hydro therapy pool. In short she could alleviate any burden Kellie had and ensure that her life was rewarding and worthwhile. This dog had a rich life ahead of her still; she had so much to give, she was happy and there was really no reason to euthanize her. Jean's note was imploring.

When the daughter finally replied, it was to report her deep love for Kellie but to let Jean know that she had had her put to sleep.

Jean was devastated. Never had this happened to her before. She felt that she had failed Kellie and she found the needless execution of this cheerful little soul too much to bear. It started to affect her very deeply and in desperation, she wrote to me to ask for meaning in all of this. I found the situation cruel and deeply saddening and had to ask Michael how to respond. Here is his reply:

"The relationships between humans and animals are of greater significance than you can possibly imagine. When our lives are interwoven with theirs it is because of the learning opportunities that present themselves, both for us and for them. If you were to see each other in your true soul forms, you are identical and your supremacy over them as beings is both a falsehood and an illusion. Particularly in the case of dogs, where your lives can be so synergistic, what you do to them you literally do to yourselves.

Agreements for learning are made between beings before they ever incarnate. When such agreements are created, a host of angels act throughout the party's lives with the sole purpose of ensuring that those agreements are enabled i.e. that the events surrounding them happen. This does not mean however that the outcome is ever certain. Agreements can be fraught with risk and hardship. It is usually the animals who will assume the role of the recipient of pain, anguish, torment and grief for the sake of humans. Often their commitment to you far outweighs what you do for them.

In this unfortunate situation there is a three way learning pact that exists between Kellie, the owner's daughter and the 'caregiver'. The former light being had agreed to assume the role of the sufferer in order to provide learning opportunities the latter. Specifically these would have involved recognizing the divine in this creature and subjugating their own ego based third dimensional needs to those of the dog. In so doing they presented themselves with an opportunity to progress as beings of spirit and acquire an element of humanity that went beyond the basic protestations of their love.

In all things there is the need for action. Expression of intention or belief that is not matched with a proportionate commitment in the physical is empty and without purpose. Sadly, both of these beings failed in their learning. The outcome for them both, should there not be a redressing of the situation in this lifetime (which is very unlikely), will be that this issue will reoccur for them; the learning opportunity will present itself as many times as is required until the point is understood. However, this does not mean to say that it will reoccur in anything like the same way. These circumstances were if anything, for them at least, a most favourable way to partake of the learning.

Kellie has played her part admirably in this situation and will progress in her journey without question. She will reincarnate in a matter of linear months where her sacrifice on their behalf will be greeted with a far more beneficial set of living circumstances. She need suffer no more in this cycle of progression. She is very close to achieving the balance levels necessary for a dog to ascend and transition to the next phase of living."

A few weeks later I was running a balance workshop. As part of the process, the participants were identifying the beliefs and values that they held that had an impact on the way in which they lived their lives. Each individual in turn revealed their attitudes and then we explored any potentially unbalancing attributes of their beliefs. One person relayed the fact that they believed it to be enormously inappropriate that people cared so strongly about animals when there were children suffering in the world. The view met with a great deal of sympathy from the fellow participants.

I was immediately reminded of Michael's words, but he wished to add in the following way:

"Each and every individual who walks the earthly planes needs to understand the true nature of their relationship with all that is around them. It is a part of their ascension pathway. In every aspect of your interactions with the other elements of the planet there is a need for a balance in co-existence. In respect to that which you go through with animals, the total subjugation of species and the dominance of other beings is in denial of the synergies that should exist between you. In the case of domesticated animals, all will spend lifetimes interrelating with other species. It is an inescapable feature of existence. Only when you have learnt to recognise them for what they are, have honoured them as they honour you, and have accepted that they are as you, will progress be made."

The group sat in stunned silence until one person said: "Does that mean I have to get a dog?"

In the dog house

In less than three years we had tripled the number of dogs we shared our lives with; but I have not yet shared what became of our cats.

Sadly Rittee died only months after we moved here. He had been slowing down for some time; after all, he was eighteen. Although our arrival in Canada gave him a temporary new lease of life, but without any warning, rapidly failing kidneys overtook him. With much regret we decided to put him out of his pain. Sasha survived him by over a year before she too succumbed to old age. She was nineteen. When we discovered her body, Indy was trying to lick her back to life, but even his mighty energies were to no avail.

Michael let us know that they had been soul travellers together and that Sasha's ultimate departure had been the choice of her higher self, at the instigation of Rittee who was impatient for them to move on together!

Some months later I was visited in an exceptionally vivid dream by the higher selves of the pair of them. They wanted to let me know that they had reincarnated and they expressed their gratitude for the lives that they had with us. The dream was an astounding experience that I was happy to share with Sharon. We both took great comfort in it.

It might appear as if the ever encroaching dog presence has been an entirely welcome one? Perhaps I hadn't emphasised the stress and difficulty it caused. We never, ever intended to get more than one when we invited Kaiti into our lives. Had it not been for her Shar Pei mind tricks, I have little doubt that we would not have extended our pet family in so ridiculous a way. But where these things are concerned, soul contracts and channelled information managed to suppress even our strongest wills. Initially Sharon resisted more dogs quite strongly and it is only after the twelve years that this strange story has gone on for that she has grown to accept it as the inevitability that only soul contracts can be. Since we arrived in Canada, not one dog has been allowed entry into our lives without regret that there is a need for another. Not one dog has failed to give us one hundred times more joy than the misgivings their arrival caused.

In tandem with, but not because of the arrival of the dogs and our spiritual journey, my work in the 'third dimensional' realms has become almost nonexistent. Despite being a highly qualified and vastly experienced development professional, as well as a former bestselling author, it is as if I have become invisible. Whereas formerly, clients beat a path to my door, without apparent rhyme or reason, my skills are no longer in demand. The reputation and accolades that I had earned are of little consequence.

You may think that this would be a bitter pill to swallow? Oddly, it is not. Financial security is a thing of the past and the pressure of providing for our extended dog family is an ever present feature of our lives. But Archangel Michael made it quite clear that our path was the one we now walk and that all that had gone before was merely preparation for what was to come. Although I won't pretend that accepting this came easily, now that we do, we find that our happiness and contentment has grown by exponential leaps and bounds.

The experience of living with so many dogs defies description and the revelation of the extent of our ownership normally meets with incredulity, particularly when people learn that they *all* live in the house with us! We know that some people think we are totally stupid while others envy the opportunities afforded to us to go through our lives with such amazing creatures.

Since we moved to Canada, Sharon's parents have not felt able to visit us. Despite the fact that they miss their grandchildren, we suspect that the prospect of having to face so many dogs puts them off totally. And they currently believe that we only have twelve! We daren't tell them the truth. My parents have come over twice now and despite initial misgivings, my cat loving mother has come to enjoy the experience of the dogs a great deal. She particularly loves to sit on the front porch on a warm evening with them spread all around her, and has even expressed a desire that they should have one of their own. "We've got a couple spare you can have" I joke!

Walking the dogs is a little different from our UK days. We have merely to open the door and they can run about to their heart's content. We extended the fence line to encompass another acre of our land and even the fastest of the dogs now takes two minutes to race around the perimeter. The space within is a treed dog wonderland, full of exciting smells and obstacles to chase around. With such freedom, they are quite well exercised. Only the older ones, particularly Kaiti, Pippa, Ktuu and Saffy prefer to spend most of their days indoors. The younger ones come and go on an almost constant basis and we often wish we had a dollar for each time we open an outside door for them during the course of a day.

On our hikes, we are spoilt for choice with who to take. We operate a rota to ensure that they all get regular outings that are appropriate to their age and ability. If we're doing crystal planting, we have to take avatars for their energetic benefits. Indy is always a strong candidate because he can be walked off the lead without needing to worry about him running away. Dougal is really bad news because he pulls so much and after fifteen kilometres, that can start to wear a little. Briony gets stressed going anywhere in the car, and despite the fact that she loves a good walk, she'll dribble copiously all the journey there. The Huskies are surprisingly good to walk with, but only Cinnda goes off leash.

In the long winters, the Husky's coats are ideal for coping with the deep snow. They move like snow ploughs and create deep trenches that the others follow them through in convoys. It is very funny to watch. The hounds come back in with packs of snow the size of golf balls attached to their fur. Sometimes it's so bad that we have to put them in the bath to thaw them out. Only Kaiti and Pippa don't have the right coats to withstand the extreme minus temperatures that we sometimes experience. On occasion they will go out and rush back in again in seconds and then need to warm up in front of a blazing open fire.

We are often asked how we manage in giving affection to so many dogs and the answer is that you develop highly creative methods of delivering coat rubs, scratches, massages and tickles in multi-faceted ways. Use of hands, head and feet simultaneously is not uncommon. They do get very jealous of one another when they are not the recipients of attention, some more than others. Lara hates it if any dog gets attention and she does not, and she'll sulk or even nip you on the bottom to alert you to her presence. Pippa's tactic is to force herself in between you and whatever dogs you *were* stroking to make sure that she gets more than her fair share. Ktuu leans her whole body weight against you so that she's unmissable. We have learnt to be as fair as we can be.

Although eighteen sounds a lot, after the initial flurry of excitement that awaits any new arrival, it is possible to be in our house and not really register that we have more than a couple of pets. This is because they spread out over the three floors and the outdoors. It is only at mealtimes that they all come together and this can be wild! With the exception of the special diet candidates (Kaiti and Saffy) all of our dogs eat the bones and raw food diet. This came about because when we were intending to get a Leonberger from Deborah, she insisted that we must feed the B.A.R.F. diet to the dog as a term of the purchase agreement. When we researched the benefits to the dogs, we willingly agreed and since then have fed ours on nothing else. They love it and at mealtimes (which they try to dictate) they all gather to receive whatever they are being given at that time. Most of the dogs sit patiently waiting for their turn, but the Huskies have an odd habit of bouncing up and down as if to alert us to their presence. They are also at their most talkative at this point! I make most of their treats by hand as it's so much cheaper than buying them. Liver bread and peanut butter cookies are their favourites.

You might assume that noise is a major problem but oddly enough it's not. Generally speaking, the dogs don't bark a great deal when they're outside. It is only when someone is coming to the house and they're inside that the din becomes frightful and pandemonium ensues. At these times, ear protection headphones are a good idea. Molly can be a bit of a pain, since for her, every departure from the house signals the start of the latest 'great squirrel hunt'. Her euphoria at this is always accompanied by the loudest possible baying which, in her case, could probably raise the dead. Only if she is led outside and then released will she not do this. Briony too can be noisy when she's goaded to be so. Scott and Shannon's house is several hundred metres downhill from ours. Although it's totally invisible to us, when he goes outside, Scott takes great delight in calling "Poodle" up the hill. Upon hearing this Briony will begin a feverish hullabaloo until called in. Fortunately she usually comes.

The dog's sleeping arrangements are in a constant state of evolution due to new arrivals. Currently we have Pippa and three of the BGVs sleeping in the basement family room, the four puppies are in the wetroom, Joe and Saffy sleep in the kitchen, and the remaining eight dogs are in our bedroom. The crush is only slightly alleviated by the fact that Indy and Timba spend half the night outside. Our nights seldom go on later than 6.30am and Sharon is usually the first up to deal with whatever horrendous mess they might have made in the night. With the older dogs there's often none, but the puppies are a different matter! We always swore that we would have no dog sleeping on our bed and for years the imploring looks and whines were resisted. However, returning from one of my trips to Europe, I discovered that a certain Poodle had taken up residence on my side of the bed and as a consequence, every night I have a battle with Briony. I come into the room and she immediately jumps off the bed. I go to the bathroom and on my return she is back. I put her on the floor yet in the last two years, I have never woken up without finding a Poodle snuggled up next to me.

Mercifully, we have not had too many problems with the dogs being destructive. Whilst other households can produce extensive catalogues of disasters wrought by their pets, here is ours: As a puppy, when left on her own on one occasion, Kaiti chewed a ball pen and the resulting blue ink stain on the carpet eventually resulted in the need for its replacement. Emily used to eat leather collars and got through at least half a dozen before we had the sense to switch to ones made of nylon webbing. Numerous beds have been destroyed over the years, in which action Pippa was the prime culprit. She wrecked Kaiti's beanbag bed which, up until that point, Kaiti had been very fond of and comfortable in. We've lost several rugs to undetermined culprits. Most recently, in retaliation for being left at home, but only after our return, Lara decided to chew the cover on the hot tub and did enough damage to necessitate its replacement. She wasn't even alone; it was a purely malicious act. Some angel!

As I have written this book, it is curious to note that at their chapters, each of the avatars (with the exception of Cinnda because of her fear of stairs, and the puppies because they're still in the whelping box) has come into the room and laid at my side. It is particularly unusual for Kaiti to even come downstairs, so they seem to know what's going on!

So here we are with eighteen dogs, absolutely resolute that there will be no more.

Do you believe that? Me neither.

The Spirit Dog

A few weeks ago I received an email from Jean, asking me if I could possibly help with transporting a rescue dog from the US border to our local city. I was unable to assist due to prior arrangements, but in the course of trying to help out and exchanging correspondence, Jean happened to mention that she was busy trying to rehome some sort of dog from a Native American reservation, the likes of which she had never seen before. She wondered if I'd heard of it.

Apparently its situation was fairly desperate, but being an eighteen dog household already, I was certain that we couldn't help and only gave the email a cursory glance. Besides, I knew that it wouldn't be an avatar or Michael would have mentioned it.

However, two days later Michael requested that I reread the email and I complied without hesitation or question, probably because it was late at night, or maybe because these days, I just do what he tells me!

I was surprised to find that I had totally misread the email. It wasn't a reservation dog at all, but a breed of dog called a Native American Indian Dog which I'd never heard of. I pride myself on my knowledge of dog breeds so I researched it and discovered that it was an extremely rare breed that had almost been pushed to the point of extinction, but had been 'recreated'. There were only six authorised breeders in the US and a very small population of the dogs themselves.

I looked up pictures on Google and was fascinated by what I found. I emailed Jean who I knew would still be wide awake and finishing off her numerous nightly doggie chores. She had offered to send the dog's history and pictures, so I took her up on the offer, but made it clear that we would definitely not be able to help. The photos revealed a stunning animal and a now familiar story of the hardships of a dog that finds its way into a rescue. Michael confirmed that it was not an avatar and I went to bed.

Sharon was woken from her sleep at 6.15am the next morning by a booming voice desiring to speak to her.

It was a being who introduces himself, on the odd occasions on which he visits, as Asrael. In the angelic hierarchy of beings he is what is known as a Power, a being of substantial responsibility on a trans-dimensional basis. When he first came through, about four years ago now, his arrival was heralded by six other beings who spoke with one eerily echoing voice, and we were concerned because the Archangel Azrael is known as the angel of death! He was quick to point out the difference. I have been unable to channel him for any longer than five minutes at a time and he only comes when my body is in a good place from a vibrational perspective. Afterwards I generally fall asleep because his energies are so powerful that they wipe me out.

This morning was particularly unusual because I was asleep and the channelling began whilst I was unconscious! His voice has enough force to fill a room and deafen you, so when a mighty and booming voice burst through my lips and announced "Good morning" so loudly that Sharon was roused from her fitful slumbers with a start, she sat bolt upright and struggled to get her faculties together. She recognised the voice instantly and was well aware of the need to listen carefully. He gives no preamble and there is nothing that suggests he's prepared to be discursive:

"You are already familiar with the nature and being of the avatars that live amongst you. You are cognoscent of the differences between their essence and those of the other creatures whom you would think of as dogs. One type may be regarded as of the earth and the third dimensional planes; the others as visitors from our realms.

You have sought to make others aware of this as you have been directed (a reference to this book!) but as yet you are ignorant of another type of being that walks the planet.

This may be described as a being of pure spirit or, if you will, a spirit dog.

It is a trans-dimensional creature and as such, it is of interest to myself.

You have already been directed to a source where you may obtain one of these creatures.

264

I wish you to obtain it as it will be of service to you in your understanding of the knowledge that I have to impart.

It will accompany you in those activities that I have asked you to perform and will request of you in the future.

It will bridge the gap of understanding and fear that exists between third dimensional beings and that which is.

I am Asrael."

Within a week Kachina came to live with us.

She is unearthly and our experiences with her have only just begun.

I am directed not to write any more about her here.

I will in the future.

Footnote

A month ago I was writing another book about leadership. I had been working on it for many weeks and making at best, faltering progress. Nothing seemed to flow and I was constantly beleaguered by doubt about it. I was pressing on because an Ascended Master called El Morya had told me that writing was key to what I was supposed to be doing to fulfil my soul contract. Naturally I assumed that leadership was an important issue. After all, I had spent twenty five years of my life becoming an expert in it. There must have been a reason for such a great investment.

Then one day as I was struggling on, Michael pointed out that I was writing the wrong book.

This was the story that I was meant to tell.

It has flowed from within me with the greatest of ease and it has been a pure pleasure to write. In total, it has taken approximately one hundred hours to complete and no more. Much of it has been channelled and Michael has told me what he wanted me to say and where.

I was to tell it because there were many people who needed to understand the concepts that are introduced in it. It was impossible to tell the story of how we come to have nineteen dogs without interweaving it with concepts that affect the whole world around us. But in much the same way, everyone's life is threaded with miraculous, strange and wonderful events; if only they could see the context and hands that are at work to make it so.

Nothing that I write is new. Even if you are not acquainted with the information shared, I have no doubt that a lot of it seemed vaguely familiar in a very strange sort of way. It shouldn't be surprising because the knowledge that I have recorded here is already stored in your soul DNA anyway.

If you have got this far, it's because you're meant to. The knowledge this book recounts is part of your awakening. It is relevant for your life and although you might not understand exactly how and why right now, you will do. Over time the messages within it and the sparks ignited will become clear and obvious.

This book was written for *you* and everything that is in it is true.

I know this because an Archangel told me so.

WOULD YOU LIKE TO HELP?

When I came to propose this book to publishers, I immediately received two offers. Upon acceptance, I was quoted publication times that were up to 18 months hence.

Archangel Michael found the timing unacceptable. He requested that the work be 'self published' and marketed virally so as to bring it to the market immediately.

The major problem we had with this was funding, yet he insisted that it was the 'right way to go'.

Almost immediately our dear friends Colleen and Wanda offered to fund its publication. It is because of their support that you are able to read this today.

However, the messages within need to be spread more widely. Michael has asked that we seek to ensure global distribution for the story because of the learning it imparts.

We cannot do this alone.

If you have enjoyed reading of our journey and would like to help spread the information as Michael has requested, may we please ask that you do the following?

Tell anyone and everyone about the book.

Tell them how much you enjoyed it.

Recommend that they read it too!

In this manner, we are confident that it will quickly and easily spread all over the world.

BUT, please don't lend them your copy; ask that they buy their own.

We are desperate to raise the money to start the Avatar sanctuary that is mentioned in the story.

The more copies that are sold, the closer we come to ensuring that as many of these amazing beings as possible are given the opportunity to fulfil their promise of service if they fall upon hard times.

And by promoting awareness of all that is revealed here, we may even manage to change the world for the better along the way.

Thank you in advance for your help and kindness. It is truly appreciated.

If you would like to know more about our story, see more pictures of the dogs and find out other ways in which you can help. Please visit our website at:

www.somedogsareangels.com